THE GLORY OF CHRIST

IN MODERN ENGLISH AND WITH A STUDY GUIDE

JOHN OWEN

GODLIPRESS TEAM

© Copyright 2024 by GodliPress Team.

All rights reserved. The content contained within this book may not be reproduced, duplicated, or transmitted without direct written permission from the author or the publisher, except in the case of brief quotations embodied in critical articles or reviews.

Unless otherwise indicated, all Scripture quotations are from The ESV® Bible (The Holy Bible, English Standard Version®), © 2001 by Crossway, a publishing ministry of Good News Publishers. Used by permission. All rights reserved.

CONTENTS

About Our Revised Editions   vii
Preface   ix

1. SEEING THE GLORY OF CHRIST   1
   The Importance of Seeing This Glory   4
   The Benefits of Seeing His Glory   8
   Study Guide - Reflections   11

2. HIS GLORY AS THE ONLY REPRESENTATIVE OF GOD   13
   The Limits of Reason   16
   Ignorance of God   17
   Jesus as God's Representative   19
   The Priority of Seeing His Glory   24
   Seeking His Glory   31
   Study Guide - Reflections   35

3. THE GLORY OF CHRIST AS MAN AND GOD   37
   Think on His Glory   40
   Study the Scriptures   43
   Meditate on His Glory   46
   Think Often of Jesus   47
   Have an Attitude of Worship   50
   Study Guide - Reflections   52

4. THE GLORY OF CHRIST AS MEDIATOR   54
   The Greatness of Jesus as Mediator   56
   The Special Nature of His Mediation   58
   The Glory of Jesus in His Mediation   63

Contemplating Him	65
Study Guide - Reflections	66
5. THE GLORY OF CHRIST IN HIS LOVE	**68**
Love of the Father	68
Love of the Son	69
Contemplating His Love	73
Study Guide - Reflections	75
6. THE GLORY OF CHRIST IN HIS WORK	**77**
His Obedience	77
His Suffering	80
Study Guide - Reflections	82
7. THE GLORY OF CHRIST IN EXALTATION	**84**
From Man to Exalted One	85
The Exaltation of Christ	88
Our Duty and Privilege	89
Study Guide - Reflections	91
8. THE GLORY OF CHRIST IN THE OLD TESTAMENT	**93**
In Rituals of the Law	94
In the Song of Songs	94
In His Appearances	95
In the Prophets	96
In Metaphors	98
Study Guide - Reflections	98
9. THE GLORY OF CHRIST IN THE CHURCH	**100**
Taking On Punishment and Justice	102
The Requirement	103
Joined With the Church	104
The Glory of this Doctrine	108
Study Guide - Reflections	110

10. THE GLORY OF CHRIST TO BELIEVERS	112
Through Creation	113
Through Christians	114
The Father's Eternal Plan	118
The Gift of the Son	119
Study Guide - Reflections	122
11. THE GLORY OF CHRIST IN RESTORATION	124
An Outline of Redemption	124
Jesus' Glory in Deliverance	130
Study Guide - Reflections	134
12. DIFFERENCES BETWEEN FAITH AND SIGHT	136
Seeing Jesus by Faith	137
Seeing Jesus With Our Eyes	141
New Minds	145
New Bodies	148
A Future Hope	149
A Brief Summary	154
Study Guide - Reflections	156
13. OBSTACLES TO SEEING THE GLORY OF CHRIST	158
The Imperfection of Faith	159
Faith in Christ	170
Seeing Perfectly	178
Study Guide - Reflections	182
14. FINAL THOUGHTS	184
Differences in Perception	184
Differences in Effects	187
Final Thoughts	194
Study Guide - Reflections	195

15. PERSUASION FOR UNBELIEVERS	197
An Invitation to the Lost	198
The Urgency of His Invitation	206
Objections to His Invitation	207
What More Can You Do?	208
Why Should I Keep Trying?	209
Putting It Off	212
Too Big a Sacrifice	214
Not That Bad	216
Study Guide - Reflections	217
16. DIRECTION FOR BELIEVERS	219
Constant Spiritual Growth	226
Danger of Decay	232
A Common Condition	236
Recovering From Decay	247
The Reason for These Words	256
More Direction	257
Study Guide - Reflections	262
About John Owen	265
Bibliography	267

ABOUT OUR REVISED EDITIONS

GodliPress exists to glorify God. While we respect the profound teachings of classic Christian authors, we do not necessarily endorse all their doctrinal views. Our mission is to faithfully preserve the rich theological depth and elegance of their works while making them more accessible to modern readers.

Our updated editions include:

- The unabridged, complete text, meticulously updated for clarity.
- Modern English sentence structure and vocabulary.
- Updated organization and headings for easier navigation.
- Scripture references from the English Standard Version (ESV).
- A thoughtfully crafted Study Guide for deeper reflection and discussions.

The included Study Guide offers additional insights and thought-provoking questions designed to help you pause and reflect on what you've read, whether individually or in a group setting. It is not intended to add to or detract from the original message but rather to guide you in applying its truths.

Our hope and earnest prayer is that, through our carefully revised editions, you'll find these Christian classics easier to understand and apply. May God bless you richly through any teachings within these pages that align with the Gospel of Christ, as revealed in His inspired Word.

PREFACE

Dear Reader,

The aim of this book is to declare some of the glory of our Lord Jesus Christ that is revealed in the Bible—the main object of our faith, love, delight, and admiration. Unfortunately, after our best efforts, we must say how little we can understand of him! His glory is incomprehensible, and his praises are unspeakable. Some things an illuminated mind may understand, but what we can express is even less than nothing. For those who have forsaken the only true guide by attempting to be wiser than Scripture revelation through their imagination (as many have done), they have questioned his authority without knowledge, speaking of things they do not understand, and have no substance or spiritual food of faith in them.

That real view we might have of Jesus and his glory in this world by faith—however weak that knowledge is which we gain through revelation—is to be preferred above all other wisdom, understanding, or knowledge. So, Paul, a competent judge in these things, says, "I have suffered the loss of all things and count them as rubbish, in order that I may gain Christ" (Phil. 3:8). The person who does not has no part in him.

The revelation of Jesus in the Gospel is far greater, more glorious, and more filled with God's wisdom and goodness than all of creation can know and contain. Without this knowledge, people's minds are still wrapped up in darkness and confusion even though they pride themselves in their inventions and discoveries.

So, it deserves serious thought, meditation, and diligence to understand them. If our future happiness consists in being where he is and seeing his glory, what better preparation can we have than to constantly contemplate that glory in the revelation of the Gospel right now? And in seeing it, we may be gradually transformed into the same glory.

I will not apologize for writing this, first as intended to help my own mind, then for the benefit of a local church. Reading this, some may be called to live their Christian lives more diligently than before as they receive directions for doing so, while some may be motivated to share their light and knowledge for the benefit of others. This preface is to briefly show the necessity and use, in life and death, of seeing Jesus' glory.

Contemplating Jesus' Glory

Individual motives for diligently carrying out this duty will be emphasized later, but these are a few general things to look at. For those not immersed in sensual pleasures—not drowned by the love of this world, and who have any proper thought about their own nature, being, and end—they are under the highest obligation to contemplate Jesus and his glory. Without this, they will never find true rest or satisfaction in their minds. He is the only source of joy that mankind can boast about.

He Lifts Us Up

Jesus, who took on our backsliding nature, is exalted above the whole creation. Our original nature, passed on from Adam and Eve, was crowned with honor and dignity. It was made in the image of God, entrusted with dominion over the earth, and made the center of excellence, beauty, and glory. But it was separated from these and made naked by sin, then laid groveling in the dust from where it came from. "You are dust, and to dust you shall return" (Gen. 3:19). This was its righteous doom. And all its inner senses were invaded by deformed lusts—everything that contrasts God, whose image it had lost. So, it became the contempt of angels, the dominion of Satan. As the enemy of creation, he never had a place to reign in except for the fallen nature of man. There was nothing more despicable and corrupt; its glory was completely gone. It had lost its closeness with God, which was its honor, and fell from him more than all the creatures, except for the demons—

this was its shame. In this state, it was left to perish eternally.

In this condition—lost, poor, cursed—the Lord, the Son of God, found our nature. In condescension and compassion, sanctifying a portion to himself, he took it to be his own, in a holy, indescribable existence, in his own person. This same nature, so fallen into the worst misery, is exalted above the whole creation of God. For in that very nature, God has "seated him at his right hand in the heavenly places, far above all rule and authority and power and dominion, and above every name that is named, not only in this age but also in the one to come" (Eph. 1:20-21, Ps. 8:3–8).

This is the greatest privilege we have among all the creatures—we may glory in, and value ourselves on it. Those who use this nature to satisfy their sensual lusts and pleasures—who think that its happiness and abilities are in their satisfaction, along with the other temporary worldly desires—are satisfied with abandoning God. But those who have received the light of faith and grace and understand the being and end of that nature in which they share, rejoice in its deliverance, into that glorious exaltation received in Jesus. Then our thoughts of him will be refreshing to our souls. Let us take care of ourselves because the glory of our nature is safe in him.

He Secures Us

In him, the relationship of our nature to God is eternally secured. We were created in a covenant relationship with God. Our nature was connected to him in friendship, likeness, and satisfaction. But the bond of this relationship was quickly broken by our defection. Our nature was morally distant from God and hostile toward him—the depth of misery. But God, in his wisdom and grace, planned to recover it and bring it back to himself. He would do it in a way that would make it impossible to ever be a separation between them anymore. Heaven and earth may pass away, but there will never be a break in the union between God and our nature again. He did it by taking it into a union with himself in the person of the Son. The fullness of the Godhead physically lived in humanity, substantially and eternally. So, its relationship with God was eternally secured. There are two wonderful mysteries I want to point out here:

1. Our nature is capable of this glorious exaltation and subsistence in God. No creature could imagine how omnipotent wisdom, power, and goodness, could motivate themselves to make this happen. It is a mystery that intrigues angels and will be admired by the church for all eternity. What mind can conceive, what tongue can express, who can sufficiently admire, the wisdom, goodness, and condescension of God in this? Since he has offered us this glorious object of our faith and meditation, how terrible and foolish if we neglect it and think of other things!
2. This is also an indescribable pledge of the love of God to us. He will only accept us in relation to himself in the man Christ Jesus because of our personal union with him. Yet, in this, he has given a wonderful pledge of his love and

valuation of our nature. "For surely it is not angels that he helps, but he helps the offspring of Abraham" (Heb. 2:16). And this kindness extends unto our persons as participants of that nature. For he designed this glory unto the man Christ Jesus, that might be the firstborn of the new creation, that we might be made conformable unto him according to our measure; and, as the members of that body of which he is the head, we are a participant in this glory.

He Is Victorious

It is he in whom our nature has been carried successfully and victoriously through all the oppositions that it is liable unto, and even death itself. But that glory I will explain distinctly in its proper place later, and therefore will here pass it by.

He Is in Heaven

He has given us a pledge that we will be able to live in this place of light, which is far above what we can see now. On earth, we live in temples of clay, that are "crushed like the moth" (Job 4:19). We cannot be elevated to even live one foot above the earth we walk on. The heavenly stars we see are too great and glorious for us to live on. We are as grasshoppers in our own eyes, at least in comparison to those gigantic beings, and they seem to be in places that would immediately swallow up and extinguish us. So, how can we think of being carried and exalted above them all? How can we have everlasting life in places more glorious than the universe? What capacity is there in our nature of such a habitation? But Jesus has given us a pledge in himself. Our nature in him passed through these visible heavens and is exalted far above them. Its eternal habitation is in the blessed place of light and glory, and he has promised that where he is, there we will be forever.

The Comfort of Christ

There are many other encouragements to incite us to diligently do what we are speaking of—contemplating Jesus' glory in his person, work, and grace. I want to focus here on the unique advantage that we gain in doing this: it will carry us cheerfully, comfortably, and victoriously through life and death, and all hardships.

As for this present life, we know what we face here. Temptations, afflictions, changes, sorrows, dangers, fears, sickness, and pains. On the other hand, we have all our earthly desires, refreshments, and comforts that are uncertain, temporary, and unsatisfactory—corrupted by sin. Everything has the root of trouble and sorrow in it. Some live in lack, poverty, and hardship all their lives, and some are never free from pain and sickness. These are magnified by the catastrophic season we are in. Every nation is filled with confusion, disorder, danger, distress, and trouble; wars and rumors of wars abound, with signs of approaching judgments; distress among nations, and men's hearts failing in fear when they see what is happening around them.

As the Bible says, there is:

No peace to him who went out or to him who came in, for great disturbances afflicted all the inhabitants of the lands. They were broken in pieces. Nation was crushed by nation and city by city, for God troubled them with every sort of distress (2 Chron. 15:5-6).

In the meantime, the deeds of wicked men aggravate the troubles of life even more; the terrible sufferings of those who follow their consciences, and divisions and hatred between Christians.

Christians and non-believers complain about the shortness, vanity, and miseries of human life. I will not look at this, since my focus is the relief that we can have against all these evils so that we do not collapse because of them and may have the victory over them.

This is what Paul is talking about:

We are afflicted in every way, but not crushed; perplexed, but not driven to despair; persecuted, but not forsaken; struck down, but not destroyed." But for this cause "we do not lose heart. Though our outer self is wasting away, our inner self is being renewed day by day. For this light momentary affliction is preparing for us an eternal weight of glory beyond all comparison, as we look not to the things that are seen but to the things that are unseen. For the things that are seen are transient, but the things that are unseen are eternal. (2 Cor. 4:8-18)

Seeing by faith things that are not seen, things spiritual and eternal, will remove all our hardships, make our burdens light, and preserve our souls from collapsing. The glory of Jesus is the center of all this, because we see the glory of God himself "in the face of Jesus Christ" (2 Cor. 4:6). The person who finds refuge in contemplating this glory will be carried above the perplexing prevailing sense of any of these evils.

It is a terrible life when people scramble for temporary relief from their hardships. There is a remedy and cure—the only ointment for all our diseases. Whatever pressures, urges, and confuses us, if we can retreat in our minds to see this glory, and find our interest in it, comfort and support will be given to us. Wicked people, in their distress, are like a "tossing sea; for it cannot be quiet" (Isa. 57:20). Others are heartless and depressed—with secret agony because of God's ways, especially when they see others doing well. The best of us can become tired and want to give up when these things press down on us for so long without a prospect of relief. This is the stronghold these prisoners find themselves in. Only in the contemplation of Jesus' glory, they find rest for their souls.

His Glory Brings Perspective

When we contemplate Jesus' glory, we see how small and insignificant all these things are that cause our troubles and distress. For they all grow from this root of an overestimation of temporary things. We must realize that all things on earth are transitory and perishing, only affecting our physical bodies (maybe even killing them)—they have nothing truly substantial in them. Unless we see that Jesus has much better things for us, we will spend our lives in fear, sorrow, and distractions. One real view of the glory of Christ and our share in it, will bring relief in this matter. What are all the things of this life? What is the good or evil of them compared to this transcendent glory? When we understand it, our minds fixed on it, and our desires reach for the joy it offers, then we will be ready to combat and overcome pain, sickness, arrows, fears, dangers, and death. Knowing these are external, temporary, and passing away, we fix our minds on those things eternal and filled with incomprehensible glory.

His Glory Calms the Mind

People's minds are often thrown into confusion by their troubles, tossed up and down, and distressed with emotion and passion. The Psalmist was like this in his distress and says, "Why are you cast down, O my soul, and why are you in turmoil within me?" (Ps. 42:5). The mind is its own worst enemy. It releases its passions of fear and sorrow, which act in many confusing thoughts until it is completely carried away of its own power. But in this state, thinking of the glory of Christ will restore and compose the mind, bringing it into a calm, quiet attitude, where faith can say to the winds and waves of infected passions, "Peace! Be still!" and they will obey it (Mark 4:39).

His Glory Shows Us His Love

It is the way of expressing a sense of God's love to our hearts which is where we ultimately find rest in the midst of all the troubles of this life (Rom. 5:2–5). It is the Spirit of God who communicates a sense of this love to us, it is "poured into our hearts through the Holy Spirit" (Rom. 5:5). However, there are also things we need to do, so we can be ready and available to receive these transmissions of love. One of the main ones is the contemplation of the glory of Christ and of God the Father in him. This is the season and method that the Holy Spirit will give a sense of God's love to us, causing us to "rejoice with joy that is inexpressible and filled with glory" (1 Pet. 1:8). This will be shown later in the book. It lifts the minds and hearts of Christians above all the troubles of this life and is the sovereign cure that will expel all the poison that confuses and enslaves their souls.

Comfort in Death

There is an advantage we can have in this practice in terms of death—constant contemplation of Jesus' glory will carry us cheerfully and comfortably into and through it. Living in constant expectation of dying, as I have become accustomed lately, I will share a few of my thoughts and reliefs about death.

There are some things we are required to do, so we are able to encounter death cheerfully, constantly, and victoriously. Without these, I have known gracious people who have lived in the bondage of fearing death all their days. We do not know how God will deal with our minds and hearts in that season and trial, because he acts toward us in sovereignty.

These are the things he requires of us in our duty:

Surrender Your Soul

In faith, we surrender and commit our departing souls into his hands to receive, keep, and preserve them, and also to bring them into a state of rest and happiness.

The soul is now parting with all things on earth forever. None of the things it has seen, heard, or enjoyed can remain with it one more hour or take one step with it in the journey it is busy in. It must launch into eternity by itself. It is entering an invisible world that it does not know of except what it has received by faith. No one has come from the dead to inform us of the state of the other world. God seems to hide it from us on purpose so that we have no evidence of the manner of things in it, only what is given to faith by revelation. So, those who died and were raised again from the dead like Lazarus probably knew nothing of the invisible state. This made a great emperor who was near death, cry out, "O poor, trembling, wandering soul, into what places of darkness and defilement art thou going?" (Henderson, n.d.).

What happens for those few moments as we die and are still in this world? Are we completely wiped out? Is death the destruction of our whole being, so there is nothing left after we die? Some say we wander up and down the world, under the influence of other powerful spirits that rule in the air, visiting tombs and lonely places, and sometimes appearing as impressions of those more powerful spirits. This is what they imagine from the story about Samuel and the witch of Endor, and is commonly believed in Catholicism, in line with their imaginary doctrine of purgatory. Or is it a state of universal misery and grief, incapable of comfort or joy? Let them think what they want because they only know the comfort or joy from their senses in this life—they can look for nothing else. Whatever the state of this invisible world, the soul can do nothing of its own after it leaves the body. It knows it is completely at the disposal of another.

No one can comfortably die except in having that faith which enables them to surrender and give up their departing souls into God's hand, who is the only one that can receive it, and bring it to a place of rest and happiness. That is why Paul says, "But I am not ashamed, for I know whom I have believed, and I am convinced that he is able to guard until that day what has been entrusted to me" (2 Tim. 1:12).

Jesus is our best example. He surrendered his spirit into the hands of his Father, to be owned and preserved by him, in its state of separation: "Father, into your hands I commit my spirit!" (Luke 23:46). The Psalmist made a similar statement in his condition (Ps. 31:5). But the faith of Jesus—what he believed and trusted in surrendering his spirit into God's hand—is expressed fully in Psalm 16.

I have set the Lord always before me; because he is at my right hand, I shall not be shaken. Therefore my heart is glad, and my whole being rejoices; my flesh also dwells secure. For you will not abandon my soul to Sheol, or let your holy one see corruption. You make known to me the path of life; in your presence there is fullness of joy; at your right hand are pleasures forevermore. (Ps. 16:8-11)

He left his soul in the hand of God, confident that it would not suffer evil in its separation but be brought again with his body into a blessed resurrection and eternal glory. So, Stephen surrendered his soul, departing under violence, into Jesus' hands. When he died, he said, "Lord Jesus, receive my spirit" (Acts 7:59).

This is the last victorious act of faith, conquering its last enemy, death. This is why the soul says,

> You are now leaving time to eternity. Everything about you is slowly fading and will suddenly disappear. The things you are entering into are still invisible, which "eye has not seen, ear heard, nor entered into the heart of man to conceive." Now, with peace and confidence, give up yourself to the sovereign power, grace, truth, and faithfulness of God, and you will find assured rest and peace.

Jesus is the one who immediately receives the souls of those who believe in him. We see it in the example of Stephen. What can be a greater encouragement to surrender into his hands, than a daily contemplation of his glory, in his person, his power, his exaltation, his work, and his grace? Who can believe in him, belong to him, and yet be afraid to commit their departing spirit to his love, power, and care? In our dying moments, we will see by faith heaven opened, and Jesus standing at the right hand of God, ready to receive us. This added to the love which all Christians have for Jesus, intensified by contemplating his glory and desiring to be with him, will strengthen and keep our minds on surrendering our souls into his hand.

Be Willing to Leave the Body

We are required to be ready and willing to part with the flesh that clothes us and with everything useful and desirable in it. The alliance, relationship, friendship, and union between the soul and the body are the greatest and closest among created beings. There is nothing like it—nothing equal to it. The union of three persons in the one single divine nature, and the union of two natures in one person of Christ, are infinite, indescribable, and beyond comparison. But among created beings, the union of these two essential parts of the same nature in one person is wonderful. It is not found in any other creatures.

Angels are pure, immaterial spirits, but have nothing in them or belonging to their essence that can die. Animals have nothing in them that can live when their bodies die. The soul of an animal cannot be preserved in a separate condition—it is nothing but a body in an act of its material powers.

Only the nature of man, in all the works of God, is capable of this. Its essential parts are separated by death, the one continuing to exist in its special powers in a separate state or condition. The powers of the whole nature, soul, and body together, are all scattered and lost by death. But the powers of one essential part—the soul—are preserved after death in a more perfect state than before. This is unique to human nature, a participant of heaven and earth—the perfection of angels above, the imperfection of the animals below. There is only one difference: Our participation in the heavenly, spiritual perfections of the angelical nature is for eternity; our participation in the imperfections of the creatures here below is only for a season. God designed our bodies for such a glorious refinement at the resurrection, that they will have no more alliance with that beastly nature that perishes forever. We will be like angels, or equal to them (Matt. 22:30). Our bodies will no longer be capable of doing things that are common to us now on earth.

This is the superiority of the nature of man. The atheist Epicureans believed that as one dies, so dies the other. They all have one breath so that a man has no pre-eminence above a beast. All go to one place. All are of the dust, and all turn to the dust again.

A very wise man agreed that when it comes to their bodies, it is for a season where we participate in their nature, but there is a difference: "Who knows whether the spirit of man goes upward and the spirit of the beast goes down into the earth?" (Ecc. 3:21).

Unless we know this and consider the different states of the spirit of men and animals, we cannot be delivered from this atheism. Thinking about it further will help us. They die in the same way, and their bodies also return to the dust for a season, but the animal has no spirit, no soul, except what dies with the body and goes to the dust. If they had, their bodies must also be raised again, otherwise death would produce a new race of creatures for eternity. But mankind has an immortal soul, a heavenly spirit, which, when the body goes in the dust for a season, ascends to heaven (where the guilt of sin and the curse of the law no longer intervene), and is there to exist in happiness and holiness.

But, because of this unique relationship between the soul and body, it is against being separated. The soul and body are naturally and necessarily unwilling to separate, where one will no longer exist, and the other does not know how it will survive or be. The body clings to the soul, and the soul enjoys this embrace.

Unless we can overcome this tendency, we can never die comfortably or cheerfully. We would rather choose to be "clothed, so that our mortality may be swallowed up by life" (2 Cor. 5:4). We want the clothing of glory to come on our whole nature, soul, and body, without separation. But if this is not so, then Christians must conquer this inclination by faith and views of Jesus' glory, to gain a desire for this end. This is why Paul says, "My desire is to depart and be with Christ, for that is far better" than to stay here (Phil. 1:23).

It is not an ordinary desire, not the one that works in me now and then, but a constant, habitual tendency, working in passionate desires. And what does he desire? It is "to depart" out of this body, from this temple, to leave it for a season. But it consists of the separation of the present state of his being, that it is no longer what it is. How is it possible that a person can have such an inclination, readiness, and desire for separation? It is from a view in faith of Christ and his glory because then the soul is satisfied that to be with him is way better than its present state and condition.

The person that will die comfortably, must be able to say within himself and to himself,

Die, then, you frail and sinful flesh: "dust you are, and to dust you shall return." I surrender you up to the righteous doom of the Holy One. Yet herein also I give you into the hand of the great Refiner, who will hide you in your grave, and purify you from all your corruption and evil inclinations. There is no other way. After a long sincere effort to put all sin to death, I find it will never be absolutely perfect, except by this going into the dust. You will not be a residence anymore for the smallest remains of sin for eternity, nor block my soul toward God.

So, rest in hope, because God, in his appointed season, when he desires to do the work of his hands, will call you, and you will answer him out of the dust. Then he will, by his almighty power, not only restore you to pristine glory, like the first creation, when thou were the pure workmanship of his hands, but enrich and clothe you with inconceivable privileges and advantages. Do not be afraid or reluctant. Go into the dust, rest in hope because you will stand in your lot at the end of the days.

To enable us in this is that view and consideration of Jesus' glory because the one who possesses all that glory experienced this separation of nature as we will.

Submit to His Timing

We must be ready to submit to the times and seasons when God wants us to depart and leave this world. Many think they will be willing to die when their time comes, but they have many reasons to hope and desire that it is not yet, which is from fear and aversion to death. Some desire to live so that they may see more of that glorious world of God for his church, which they believe he will accomplish. So, Moses prayed that he might not die in the wilderness, but go over Jordan, and see the promised land, and that mountain and Lebanon, the seat of the church, and of the worship of God. Yet God saw fit to deny him. And this denial of the request of Moses is helpful for us. Others may think they have some work to do in the world, supposing it concerns the glory of God and the good of the church. So, they want to be spared for a season.

Paul did not know whether it was not best for him to stay a while longer in the flesh because of this reason. David often hated the season of death because of the work that he had to do for God in the world. Others rise no higher than their own personal interests or concerns for themselves, their families, relationships, and goods in this world. They want to see these things in a better or more settled condition before they die, and then they will be willing to do so. But it is the love of life that lies at the bottom of all these desires. But no one can die cheerfully or comfortably if they do not live in the constant surrender of the time and season of their death to the will of God. Our times are in his hand, at his sovereign disposal. His will in all things must be obeyed. Without this decision and surrender, no one can enjoy any solid peace in this world.

Prepare for the Trials of Death

When death approaches, it brings special trials to us. Unless we are prepared for them, they will keep us under bondage, afraid of death. There are long illnesses, burning fevers, and other pains in us. There is also the sword, fire, torture, and persecution. Those who have been freed from all fear of death, as a separation of nature, who have looked on it as wonderful and desirable, have still thought in their minds about how death would come. They have sincerely desired that the bitterness of the cup be taken away. To rise above all confusion that comes from these things is part of our wisdom in dying daily. We must always be ready in character and duties necessary for this. This is a constant surrender of ourselves in everything to the sovereign will, pleasure, and disposal of God. "May he not do what he will with his own?"

- Is this not right?
- Is his will in all things not infinitely holy, wise, just, and good?
- Does he not know what is best for us, and what works best to his own glory?
- Does he not do this alone?

To live in faith is to know that if God calls us to anything terrible to our nature, he will give us spiritual strength and patience to enable us to endure it, if not with ease and joy, then with peace and calm beyond our expectation. Many have experienced those things that seemed to be overwhelming and heavy to bear when strength has been received from above to encounter them. In this case, we must frequently compare these things with those which are eternal: the misery which we are freed from and that happiness which is prepared for us.

None of the things we have insisted on—the surrender of a departing soul into the hand of God, a willingness to lay down this flesh in the dust, or a readiness to comply with the will of God with the time and way death comes—can be attained without a prospect of that glory that gives us a new state far better than what we leave behind or depart from. We cannot have this, whatever we think, unless we see the glory of Christ now on earth. An anxiety of the future manifestation of it in heaven will not relieve us, if we do not know what it is, and what it consists of—if we do not discover it in this life. This is what will make everything easy and pleasant for us, even death, as it is a method to bring us to its full enjoyment.

1

SEEING THE GLORY OF CHRIST

Father, I desire that they also, whom you have given me, may be with me where I am, to see my glory that you have given me because you loved me before the foundation of the world.
—John 17:24

When the Old Testament high priest entered the holy place on the day of atonement, he took sweet incense from the golden table and fire from the altar. Walking through the veil, he put the incense on the fire in the container until the smoke covered the ark and the mercy seat (Lev. 16:12-13). This was to offer God a sweet-smelling fragrance from the sacrifice.

When Jesus, the great High Priest, entered "into holy places [not] made with hands," the heavens were filled with a cloud of incense, a sweet perfume of his intercession, just like the incense offered in the Old Testament (Heb. 9:24). With the same eternal fire that he became a sacrifice for the atonement of our sin, his heart burned for his church to also benefit from, as we see in the words of his prayer: "to see my glory."

He respected his own glory and its manifestation, which he asked the Father for in John 17:4-5. But here, it is more for the advantage, benefit, and satisfaction of his disciples. For this was the aim of the glory given to him. When Joseph revealed himself to his brothers, he told them to tell his father of all his "glory in Egypt," (Gen. 45:13). He did not do this to show off his own glory, but for the satisfaction his father would take knowing it. This is what Jesus wants for his disciples—to satisfy them forever.

This is what he prayed for, to give them satisfaction and nothing else. The hearts of believers are like a needle touched by a magnet that cannot rest until it points in its direction. When they are touched by the love of Jesus and are marked by it, they will always be moving and restless, until they come to him, and see his glory. The soul that is satisfied without it does not share in the power of his prayer.

One of the greatest privileges and growths for believers, in this world and in eternity, is in seeing the glory of Jesus. This is why he desires it for them in this prayer—"to see my glory"—that they may see, view, or know his glory. The reason I do not link this glorious privilege to heaven, as it usually is with this prayer, but also apply it to believers in this world, will be made clear.

In their hearts, unbelievers say, "Where is the glory?" They do not see any "form nor comeliness in him," that they desire. They look at him as Michal, Saul's daughter, did at David dancing before the ark when she despised him in her heart. They do not say, "Jesus is accursed!", but cry, "Greetings, Rabbi!" and then crucify him (1 Cor. 12:3, Matt. 26:49).

This is why we have so many incorrect opinions about his glory—some of them are very destructive, denying the "the Master who bought them," and substituting a false Jesus in his place (2 Pet. 2:1). Other people's offensive thoughts of him and his glory come through their bold, irreverent questions about his Person in Christianity. Their own answers border on blasphemy.

There has never been a time since Christianity that has seen such direct opposition to the person and glory of Jesus, as the days we live in. In the early church, there were many proud and crazy people who vented many foolish imaginations about him, which became false religions. The gates of hell in those have not prevailed against the rock on which the church is built. Just as Caesar went out alone to destroy the commonwealth, so we now have many who oppose the person and glory of Christ, pretending to be logical and reasonable people. The disbelief of the Trinity, and the incarnation of the Son of God—the sole foundation of Christianity—is so diluted in the world, that it almost has lost all its power. God, in his appointed time, will powerfully defend his honor and glory from the useless attempts of people against them.

In the meantime, it is the duty of all those who love the Lord Jesus in sincerity to testify of his divine Person and glory, because of the opposition against them.

I want to demonstrate that seeing the glory of Jesus is one of the greatest privileges and developments that

Christians are capable of in this world or the one to come. That is how we are gradually conformed to it, and then rooted in the eternal enjoyment of it. In this life, seeing his glory, we are changed or transformed into the likeness of it (2 Cor. 3:18). But in heaven, "we shall be like him, because we shall see him as he is" (1 John 3:1-2). Our present comforts and future holiness depend on this. This is the life and reward of our souls. "He that has seen him has seen the Father also" (John 14:9). For we discern the "light of the knowledge of the glory of God only in the face of Jesus Christ" (2 Cor. 4:6).

There are two ways or degrees that the Bible says we can see Jesus' glory. The one is by faith, in this world: "the evidence of things not seen;" the other is with our eyes in eternity. While we are in this world, while we are "at home in the body we are away from the Lord... we walk by faith, not by sight" (2 Cor. 5:6-7). But we will live and walk by sight in heaven and the immediate object of our faith and sight will be the Lord Jesus and his glory. Here on earth, "we see in a mirror dimly" [by faith], "but then face to face" [by sight]. "Now I know in part; then I shall know fully, even as I have been fully known" (1 Cor. 13:12).

The Importance of Seeing This Glory

Jesus' prayer that his disciples will be where he is and see his glory is the second way: vision in the light of glory. But we are not focusing on that here, as I want to look at the first way, the way of seeing his glory by faith.

Seeing His Glory in This World

No one will ever see the glory of Christ in heaven if they do not see it by faith here in this world to some degree. Grace is a necessary preparation for glory and faith for sight. Where the soul is not previously seasoned with grace and faith, it is not capable of glory or vision. Those not willing to do so, cannot desire it, no matter how much they pretend—they only deceive their own souls into thinking they do. Many will say with confidence that they desire to be with Jesus and to see his glory, but they cannot say why they want to —they only think it is better than hell. If a person pretends to desire something he has never seen or was shown to him, they only hold onto their own fantasies.

Religious churches delude themselves this way. Their worldly emotions are excited by their physical senses to delight in images of Jesus—his sufferings, resurrection, and glory above. In these things, they satisfy themselves that they have seen his glory. But these are not true representations of him or his glory in these things, and they deceive themselves.

John talks about when Jesus was with the disciples, that they saw "his glory, glory as of the only Son from the Father, full of grace and truth" (John 1:14).

What Glory Did They See, and How Did They See It?

1. It was not the glory of his secular status, as we see the glory and grandeur of earthly kings, because he had no reputation or rank, but was a

servant. He had no palace, house of entertainment, or a place to lay his head.
2. It was not his physical body, that he took on our nature, as we see the glory of a handsome or beautiful person because there was nothing desirable about him since "his appearance was so marred, beyond human semblance" (Isa. 52:14). He was seen as "a man of sorrows" (Isa. 53:2-3).
3. It was not the eternal essential glory of his divine nature, because no one can see it in this world. We do not know what we will see in heaven.
4. It was his glory, as he was "full of grace and truth" (John 1:14). They saw the glory of his person and his role in bringing grace and truth.

How Did They See This Glory?

It was by faith, and nothing else, because this privilege was given only to those who "did receive him, who believed in his name" (John 1:12). This was the glory John the Baptist saw, when he said, "Behold, the Lamb of God, who takes away the sin of the world" (John 1:29–33).

Anyone who does not see the glory of Christ here will never have any of it in heaven.

Not Able to See His Heavenly Glory

Seeing Christ in glory is too high and marvelous for us in our present condition. Its splendor and glory are too great for us to see spiritually properly now, just as looking directly at the sun will blind us instead of relieving us. There is no other way to spiritually understand what it is to see the glory of Jesus in heaven, except to see the same glory by faith in this life. Everything else is guessing and imagination.

I have read many writings of educated men about the state of future glory; some of them are filled with excellent truth and beautiful language that causes us to think about what they say. But still, reading these books, many complain that it is like looking "intently at his natural face in a mirror. For he looks at himself and goes away and at once forgets what he was like" (James 1:23-24). The things they read please and refresh for a little while, like rain in a dry season, but do not soak down to the roots of things—their power does not enter. The soul is disturbed, not edified, in thinking of future glory, when it has no foretaste, sense, experience, or evidence of what is spoken of. No one should look for anything in heaven, except for what they have experienced of it in this life. If we were convinced of this, we would be more inclined to exercise faith and love about heavenly things. Instead, we do not know what we enjoy, so we do not know what we look for.

Many people who are strangers to experiencing the beginning of glory in themselves as an effect of faith have filled their worship with images, pictures, and music, to represent that glory which they imagine is above. But there is no truth in it, because they have no experience of its power in themselves, nor do they taste its goodness through any of its first fruits in their own minds. It is only by seeing Jesus' glory by faith here in this world that we may begin to see his glory above by sight, and our hearts will be able to admire and desire its fullness.

Diligently Seeking This Glory

If we see the glory of Christ now, then the life and power of faith is active. From our faith, our love for Jesus springs. If we desire to have faith in its energy or love in its power, bringing peace and satisfaction to our souls, we must seek them this way—they will not be found any other way. In this, I live and die—in this, I bring my thoughts and emotions to the fading of all the painted wonders of this world, to the crucifying of all things here below, until they become dead to me.

Because there is no benefit in just thinking about this truth except what comes from the growth in doing it— the constant beholding of the glory of Jesus by faith— I will look at its advantages.

The Benefits of Seeing His Glory

Unless we improve the practice of seeing his glory constantly by faith, we will have no benefits in it. These are a few advantages in this practice:

1. **Made ready for heaven:** Not everyone desires or hopes for it because some are unworthy of it or excluded through sin. Everyone thinks they are ready for glory if they can get there, but it is because they do not know what it is. Music has no pleasure to those who cannot hear, and the most beautiful colors cannot be seen by the blind. It would not benefit a fish to take him

from the bottom of the cold, dark ocean and place him under the rays of the sun. It will not be refreshed for it is not capable. Heaven would not be an advantage for people who are not renewed by the Spirit of grace in this life. So, Paul gives "thanks to the Father, who has qualified you to share in the inheritance of the saints in light" (Col 1:12). The beginning here on earth, and the fullness of glory in heaven, are communicated to believers by an almighty act of the will and grace of God. But he has given us a way for us to become receptive subjects of the glory transmitted to us: beholding the glory of Jesus by faith. All our present glory consists in our preparation for future glory.

2. **Transformed into his image**: No one can see the complete glory in faith, but righteousness will come from it in a transforming power to change him "into the same image" (2 Cor. 3:18). How this is done, and how we become like Jesus by seeing his glory, we will discover as we continue.

3. **Find rest and comfort**: The constant contemplation of the glory of Jesus will give rest, satisfaction, and comfort to our hearts. Our minds are easily filled with many confusing thoughts—fears, cares, dangers, distresses, passions, and lusts—filling us with disorder, darkness, and confusion. But where the heart is focused in its thoughts and contemplation on this glorious object, it will be brought and kept in a holy, peaceful, spiritual attitude. "To set the

mind on the Spirit is life and peace" (Rom. 8:6). We do this by removing our hearts from all thoughts of things below, in comparison to the great worth, beauty, and glory of what we are talking of here (Phil. 3:7–11). Not doing this makes many of us strangers to a heavenly life; we live beneath the spiritual refreshments and satisfactions that the Gospel offers us.

4. **Be with him forever**: The sight of the glory of Jesus is the spring and cause of our everlasting happiness. "We will always be with the Lord" (1 Thess. 4:17), or "be with Christ," which is best of all (Phil. 1:23). For there we will see his glory and by seeing him as he is, we will be made like him (1 John 3:2). This is our eternal favor and happiness. The enjoyment of seeing God is called the <u>beatific vision</u>, and it is the fountain of everything our souls need for a state of happiness. The old philosophers knew nothing of this, and neither do we. God in his immense essence is invisible to our physical eyes and will be so until eternity—and also incomprehensible to our minds. For nothing can perfectly comprehend that which is infinite, but what is itself infinite. So, the only view we will have of God will always be "in the face of Jesus Christ" (2 Cor. 2:4). There the manifestation of the glory of God, in his infinite perfections, will shine into our souls and fill us with peace, rest, and glory.

We can admire these things but not understand them. But in true believers, there is a foresight and foretaste of this glorious condition. Sometimes, through the Word and Spirit, our hearts will experience the glory of God, shining in Jesus, satisfying our hearts with inexpressible joy. That is where "the peace of God, which surpasses all understanding," keeps our "hearts and… minds in Christ Jesus" (Phil. 4:7). Jesus, in believers, "the hope of glory," gives us a taste of the blessings of it through bathing our souls in the fountain of life and drinking from the rivers of pleasure at his right hand (Col. 1:27). But it is because of our own laziness and darkness that we do not enjoy more visits of this grace, and that his glory does not more shine in our hearts. Hopefully, we are motivated to diligently pursue these things.

Through the book, I will answer these questions:

1. What is the glory of Jesus we see by faith?
2. How do we see it?
3. How is it different from seeing it in heaven?

And we will attempt to answer the spouse's question asked of the daughters of Jerusalem: "What is your beloved more than another beloved, O most beautiful among women? What is your beloved more than another beloved, that you thus adjure [charge] us?" (Song. 5:9).

Study Guide - Reflections

It is interesting to see that Jesus asks for this very thing in his prayer. Besides asking God to keep and preserve them, he makes a specific request for them to be able to see his glory. Now, we know that Jesus never wasted his words by saying things without any reason or point. Even his parables were carefully constructed to convey deep spiritual matters that needed addressing. And so, when he prays for his disciples, this is one of the key things he asks for. Why? That is what John Owen proceeds to look at. If Jesus asked for it, surely we should also look into it and want to be able to see this glory.

In the original version, he used the word "behold," one that is not common in our language or frequently used. So, we have substituted "see his glory" in place of "behold his glory" for the sake of easier reading. But, as you read, bear in mind that behold is not just seeing, it is more observing, taking it all in, seeing and knowing together. With this in mind, we are not looking for a bright light or a picture of Jesus on his throne, but the knowledge of him as resurrected Lord and Savior.

1. What do you understand by the phrase "glory of Christ"?
2. How do you think it is possible to see this glory? What do we need to help us in this?
3. Why do you think Jesus prayed this just before he was about to die and leave his disciples, and not right at the beginning when he called them to follow him?
4. Is this a topic that is preached in churches these days or not? Why?
5. Have you ever seen any of Jesus' glory?
6. Which of the benefits of his glory that are listed appeals to you the most?

2

HIS GLORY AS THE ONLY REPRESENTATIVE OF GOD

The glory of Christ is the glory of the person of Jesus. So, he calls it "my glory that you have given me," which belongs to him, to his person.

The person of Jesus can be seen in two ways:

1. completely
2. in fulfilling the purpose before him

His glory is distinct and different in both of these, but still equal.

The first thing we see in the glory of the person of Jesus —God and man—is the representation of the nature of God and of the divine person of the Father. We see "the glory of God in the face of Jesus Christ" (2 Cor. 4:6). There is no other way we can know or see God because that is the way according to the Bible. The glory of God consists of the holiness of his nature and the purpose of his will, and we only have the "light of the knowledge" of these things when we see "the face" or person "of Jesus Christ."

He is "the image of God" (2 Cor. 4:4), "the radiance of the glory of God and the exact imprint of his nature" (Heb. 1:3), and "the image of the invisible God" (Col. 1:15). He is glorious as the representative of the nature of God and his will to us. Without him, it would have been hidden from us forever or been invisible to us—we would never have seen God at any time, here or in heaven (John 1:18).

In his divine person, he is the image of God. He is in the Father, and the Father in him (John 14:10). Now he is "with the Father" in the distinction of his person, his representation (John 1:1, Col. 1:15, Heb. 1:3). In his human form, he is the representative image of God to the church, (2 Cor. 4:6); without whom we will not understand the divine nature of God—he will remain the "invisible God." Only in the face of Jesus can we see his glory.

This is the original glory of Christ, given to him by his Father, and which we see by faith. He declares, represents, and makes the glory of the invisible God, his attributes, and his will, visible to all.

This is the foundation of Christianity, the rock on which the church is built, and the ground of all our hopes of salvation, life, and eternity. Everything comes down to this: the representation of the nature and will of God in the person and role of Jesus. Without this, we are lost forever. However, if this rock stands firm, the church is safe and will be victorious.

In this, Jesus is glorious. Those who cannot see his glory by faith—that he divinely represents God to us—they do not know him and end up worshiping an image they have created.

The person that cannot discern the representation of the glory of God in the person of Jesus is an unbeliever. It was the same with the unbelieving Jews and Gentiles in the Bible; they did not, they would not, and they could not see the glory of God in him, nor how he represented him. Paul talks about this:

For since, in the wisdom of God, the world did not know God through wisdom, it pleased God through the folly of what we preach to save those who believe. For Jews demand signs and Greeks seek wisdom, but we preach Christ crucified, a stumbling block to Jews and folly to Gentiles, but to those who are called, both Jews and Greeks, Christ the power of God and the wisdom of God. For the foolishness of God is wiser than men, and the weakness of God is stronger than men. (1 Cor. 1:21–25)

To not see the wisdom, power, and holiness of God in Jesus is to be an unbeliever.

Faith is giving proper credit to the glory of God (Rom. 4:20). We do not get this unless he reveals his glory to us. This is done in Jesus alone so we may glorify God in the right way. Anyone who does not acknowledge the glory of divine wisdom, power, goodness, love, and grace in Jesus is an unbeliever.

The devil's plan has always been to blind us and fill our

minds with prejudices so that we will not see his glory. This is why Paul writes:

And even if our gospel is veiled, it is veiled to those who are perishing. In their case the god of this world has blinded the minds of the unbelievers, to keep them from seeing the light of the gospel of the glory of Christ, who is the image of God. (2 Cor. 4:3-4)

The devil has used various ways and methods to deceive us through false supernatural power and wisdom so that we will be blind to the glorious light of the gospel proclaiming Jesus as the image of God. Only the mighty power of God can remove this blindness, because God, who commanded the light to shine out of darkness, has enlightened our hearts with the knowledge of the glory of God in the face of Jesus (2 Cor. 4:6). This is what true saving faith is.

The unbelieving Jews and Gentiles were all lost, and the same is true for those today who deny the divine person of Jesus because no person can ever make a perfect representation of God for us.

The Limits of Reason

Since mankind fell from God in sin, part of the punishment is that they are covered with darkness and ignorance of the nature of God.

They do not know him and have not seen him. This is why the promise was made to the church: "For behold, darkness shall cover the earth, and thick darkness the peoples; but the Lord will arise upon you, and his glory will be seen upon you" (Isa. 60:2).

Ancient philosophers tried to understand the nature of the Divine Being—its existence and attributes. They used intellectual and eloquent words to convince people, boasting that they were the wisest men in the world, but Paul says that the world in its wisdom did not know God (1 Cor. 1:21-22). He calls them atheists or people "without God in the world" (Eph. 2:12). This is because:

They had no proper guide, rule, or light to lead them into the knowledge of godly things. All they had was their own reasonings or imaginations, and they "became futile in their thinking, and their foolish hearts were darkened" (Rom. 1:21). They try and feel their way toward him in the dark, not understanding anything clearly (Acts 17:27).

Whatever they discovered about supernatural things, they were still stuck in idolatry and all kinds of sins, thinking that these could benefit them somehow as Paul clearly demonstrates in Romans 1. Jesus is the "light of men," the "light of the world;" because only in and through him can this darkness be removed—he is the "sun of righteousness" (John 1:4, Matt. 5:14, Mal. 4:2).

Ignorance of God

This darkness and ignorance of God, his nature, and his will, was where evil came into the world.

1. On this, Satan built his kingdom and throne to declare himself as "the god of this world" (2 Cor 4:4). He exalted himself through darkness

to take the place of God as the object of religious worship. Everything the Gentiles sacrificed was to devils and not to God, (1 Cor. 10:20, Lev. 17:7, Deut. 32:17, Ps. 106:37, Gal. 4:8). This is Satan's territory—the power of his kingdom in the minds of the "sons of disobedience" (Eph. 2:2). This is how he maintains his dominion throughout many nations and numerous people.

2. This is where all wickedness and confusion among people comes from. This caused the abundance of sin that God took away with a flood and the sins of Sodom and Gomorrah, which he avenged with fire from heaven. All the anger, blood, confusion, desolation, cruelty, oppression, and crime that has filled the world, taking with it the souls of people into eternal destruction, have all come from this corrupt ignorance of God.

3. We are heirs and children of this evil ignorance. It is only through infinite mercy that "the sunrise shall visit us from on high" (Luke 1:78). God could have left us to die in the blindness and ignorance of our ancestors, but by his powerful grace, he has "called you out of darkness into his marvelous light" (1 Pet. 2:9). Unfortunately, the ungratefulness of people for the glorious light of the Gospel, and the abuse of it, will end in judgment. In the Old Testament, God was known through revelation of his Word, and in worship of him. This was the glory and privilege of Israel (Ps. 147:19-20),

"He declares his word to Jacob, his statutes and rules to Israel. He has not dealt thus with any other nation; they do not know his rules" (Ps. 147:19-20). But he lived in "thick darkness," so they did not have any clear view of him (Exod. 20:21, Deut. 5:22, 1 Kings 8:12, 2 Chron. 6:1). The reason why he hid from them was to instruct them in their imperfect state because they could not comprehend the glory which would be revealed. But now, he has made himself known in Jesus, he "is light, and in him is no darkness at all" (1 John 1:5).

4. When it came to the knowledge of God, darkness covered the earth and the people, with only a twilight in the church. The day did not yet dawn, the shadows did not flee, nor did the light shine in the hearts of men. But when the "sun of righteousness" did arise in his strength and beauty, when the Son of God "manifested in the flesh," and took his place—God himself, in three distinct persons, with all the glorious properties of divine nature—was revealed to those who believed. The light of knowledge removed all the shadows in the church and shone into the darkness in the world, so no one could remain ignorant of God except for those who refused to see (John 1:5-18, 2 Cor. 4:3-4).

Jesus as God's Representative

This is where Jesus is glorious.

Jesus calls to us, saying, "Turn to me—look to me—and be saved" (Isa. 45:22). What is it that we see in him? Do we see him as the "image of the invisible God," representing him, his nature, properties, and will to us? (Col. 1:15). Do we see him as the character and the likeness of the Father, so we do not need to say, as Philip did, "Lord, show us the Father"? Because when we see him, we have also seen the Father (John 14:8-9).

If we see Jesus—God in him—we see his glory, because there he is eternally glorious. This is the glory we should long for and strive to see. And if we do not, we are still in darkness; we say we see but are blind like others. David longed and prayed to see it, even though he could only do so in part because there was an obscure representation of God's glory in the sanctuary: "O God, you are my God; earnestly I seek you; my soul thirsts for you; So I have looked upon you in the sanctuary, beholding your power and glory" (Ps. 63:1-2).

How much more should we value the view we have of his glory with open, unveiled faces (2 Cor. 3:18)?

Moses had seen the works of God which were great and marvelous, but was not satisfied, and prayed that God would show him his glory. He knew that the ultimate rest and satisfaction of the soul is not in seeing the works of God, but the glory of God himself. So, his desire made him ask, "Please show me your glory" (Exod. 33:18). And if we have the right apprehensions of the future state of happiness and holiness, we cannot but have the same desire to see more of his glory in this life.

How can we have this? Left to ourselves, with nothing but our thoughts on the immensity of the divine nature, we will come to the same conclusion as Augur had:

Surely I am too stupid to be a man. I have not the understanding of a man. I have not learned wisdom, nor have I knowledge of the Holy One. Who has ascended to heaven and come down? Who has gathered the wind in his fists? Who has wrapped up the waters in a garment? Who has established all the ends of the earth? What is his name, and what is his son's name? Surely you know! (Prov. 30:2–4)

It is only in Jesus that we can have a clear view of the glory of God and his attributes. For he is the only one appointed as the representative of God for us (John 1:18, John 14:7–10; 2 Cor. 4:6; Col. 1:15; Eph. 3:4–10; Heb. 1:3).

God's Wisdom

God's wisdom is one of the most glorious godly characteristics, a directive of all the external works of God, where the glory of all his other attributes is revealed. Job asks, "But where shall wisdom be found? And where is the place of understanding?" (Job 28:12). "Can you find out the deep things of God? Can you find out the limit of the Almighty?" (Job 11:7). Because wisdom is an essential, eternal attribute of God, we cannot fully understand it—we can only admire and worship it from where we stand. However, we can see it when it is working and its effects, for God designed them to show his wisdom. The greatest of these is the salvation of the church. Paul says:

To bring to light for everyone what is the plan of the mystery hidden for ages in God, who created all things, so that through the church the manifold wisdom of God might now be made known to the rulers and authorities in the heavenly places (Eph. 3:9-10).

If we have any interest in God, if we have any hope of seeing his glory in eternity, we must desire to see (as much as possible) the infinite wisdom of God in this life. But it is only in Jesus that we can discern it, because the Father chose him to represent it to us. All the treasures of this wisdom are hidden in him—this is the essence and form of faith. This is how Christians see the wisdom of God in Jesus, in his person and function: Christ the wisdom of God. Unbelievers do not see it (1 Cor. 1:22–24).

In seeing the glory of this infinite wisdom of God in Jesus, we also see his own glory—the glory his Father gave him. This is his glory, that only in and through him, the wisdom of God is revealed and represented to us. When God appointed him as the only way, he gave him honor and glory above all creation. We cannot deny the wisdom of God as it is shown in creation, designed by God to be enough proof against atheists and unbelievers (Rom 1:20). But when it comes to wisdom in Jesus, it cannot compare, because that is how we know God properly and live for him. To see this wisdom clearly makes Christians "rejoice with joy that is inexpressible and filled with glory" (1 Pet. 1:8).

God's Love

God's love should not just be thought of in what it does, but in its nature and character—it is God himself, because "God is love" (1 John 4:8). And a blessed revelation this is of the divine nature; it removes envy, hatred, malice, revenge, with all their fruits of rage, violence, cruelty, persecution, and murder. These are not in God's nature because he is love, which is why John says Cain did the work of the devil since he "was of the evil one and murdered his brother" (1 John 3:12).

But the question remains: How can we see this love and the glory that is in it? It is hidden in God himself. Wise philosophers who debated the topic of the love of God did not know that "God is love," and their best ideas and conclusions about it were far off the mark. Generally, people think God is easy-going and superficial as if he is like us (Ps. 50:21). Although we can learn about what love does, how it works, and its effects, if we do not know Jesus, we do not know love. There are many things that can distort our views of this love because even though "God is love," we also read that "the wrath of God is revealed from heaven against all ungodliness and unrighteousness of men," and see evidence of his anger and displeasure. How can we know and see the glory of God in this, that he is love? John gives the answer: "In this the love of God was made manifest among us, that God sent his only Son into the world, so that we might live through him" (1 John 4:9). This is the only evidence given to us that "God is love." This alone is the divine nature that has been made known to us in the mission, person, and role of the Son of God. Without this, we are in the dark about the true nature and great work of this godly love.

This is how we see the glory of Jesus. It was given to him by the Father to declare and reveal that "God is love" so "that in everything he might be preeminent" (Col. 1:18). We can see here how excellent, beautiful, glorious, and desirable he is because when we see him, we have a true representation of God because he is love. This is the most wonderful sight of God that any of us can have. Anyone who does not see the glory of Jesus this way is completely ignorant of those heavenly mysteries They do not know God or Jesus, and they do not have the Father or the Son, because they do not know the holy attributes of his nature designed by infinite wisdom for their manifestation. They do not know Jesus, because they do not see the glory of God in him. Even if they observe nature and see God's provision, and realize that there is love in him, it will not help them know that "God is love." These are the deep things of God, the wisdom of God that is a mystery to those who think and try to reason in their natural minds (1 Cor. 2:14).

The Priority of Seeing His Glory

Some people do not even consider these things, choosing to rather despise them. They are not serious about seeing the glory of God in Christ—they are unbelievers. They view him as a teacher sent by God to reveal his will and to teach us to worship. He was those things, but they say that was his only role in religion, as in Islam. They do not consider the holy attributes of his godly nature, that he is an example for angels and the church, that he is the image of the invisible God, in his person and function. They despise and mock what is said concerning them because pride and contempt of others are always the safest way to hide ignorance, otherwise, it would be strange that they openly boast of their own blindness. But these ideas are influenced by the unbelief of Jesus' godly person, causing havoc in Christianity.

To those whose minds are focused on heavenly things, I ask: Why do you love Jesus? Why do you trust him? Why do you honor him? Why do you desire to be in heaven with him? Can you give a reason for this hope that is in you, an account for why you do these things? If you cannot, all that you pretend toward him is imagination—you fight like men beating the air. Or is one of your reasons that by faith in him, you see the glory of God, with the holy attributes of his nature, that work for your salvation and favor, which would have been hidden from you forever without it? This is why Jesus is precious to those who believe (1 Pet. 2:7).

If we are spiritual, let us have the same mind and attitude. Let us make use of this privilege with rejoicing, and be carrying out this duty with diligence, because to see the glory of God is both our privilege and our duty. The duties of the Old Testament were a burden, but those of the Gospel are privileges and advantages.

A promise for the New Testament is that our "eyes will behold the king in his beauty" (Isa. 33:17). We will see the glory of Christ in all its splendor. What is this beauty of the King of saints? Is it not that God is in him, and he is the great representative of his glory to us? It is an act of faith. The glory of this privilege is that we were born in darkness, and deserved to be thrown into darkness, but are now translated into this marvelous "light of the knowledge of the glory of God in the face of Jesus Christ?" (2 Cor 4:6).

What are all the stained glories and fading beauties of this world that the devil showed our Savior from the top of the mountain? How can they compare with one view of the glory of God represented in Jesus, the glory of Jesus as his representative? The worst consequence of unbelief is that when it comes under Satan's power, it "has blinded the minds of the unbelievers, to keep them from seeing the light of the gospel of the glory of Christ," and they die spiritually (2 Cor. 4:3-4).

Jesus told the Pharisees that even with all their boasting of the knowledge of God, they still had not heard his voice or seen his form as Moses did (John 5:37). They had no real relationship with him—they had no spiritual view of his glory. It is the same with us, that even though we have some knowledge of Jesus, few of us see his glory, so, very few are transformed into his image and likeness.

Some people speak a lot about the imitation of Christ, and following his example, which is good if it was evident. But no one will ever become like him by copying his actions or without having a view or understanding of his glory because it is the only transforming power that can change them into the same image.

If we are honest, we are all failing in this regard, and many are discouraged because it has become a superstition. We do not want to take it seriously and come with a lazy attitude of engaging our minds in it.

Thoughts about this glory of Jesus are too high for us, or too hard for us, so we do not enjoy it for long. We turn away tired. Is this the reason, that we are unspiritual or naturally minded, where our minds are easily distracted and entertained by other things? This is the main cause of our unreadiness and incapacity to engage our minds in the great mysteries of the Gospel (1 Cor. 3:1–3). We do not motivate and inspire ourselves to exercise our faith in this matter diligently and seriously. This is what keeps many of us so far from the heavenly life and spiritual joy.

If we were active in this duty and in exercising our faith, our life in walking before God would be sweeter and more pleasant—our spiritual light and strength would be stronger every day—we would represent the glory of Jesus in our actions more than normal, and even death itself would be welcome to us.

Angels long to look into the glory of Jesus since the wisdom of God is made known to them through these things (1 Pet. 1:12, Eph. 3:10).

- If they diligently look into these things, why do we neglect them, especially since these things concern us more than them?
- Is Jesus glorious in our eyes?
- Do we see the Father in him?
- Do we think of the wisdom, love, grace, goodness, holiness, and righteousness of God each day, as revealing and manifesting themselves in him?
- Do we think that that the vision of this glory in

heaven we see now will be our everlasting blessing?
- Does the imperfect view which we have of it here increase our desire for the perfect sight of it above?

Is It Necessary?

To those who say they do not understand these things, because they have no bearing on life as a Christian, I have this to say:

1. Nothing is more fully and clearly revealed in the gospel than Jesus as "the image of the invisible God." The gospel shows he is the character of the person of the Father, so when we see him, we also see the Father; and that we have "the light of the knowledge of the glory of God in the face of Jesus Christ" (2 Cor. 4:6). This is the mystery and truth of the Gospel, and if it is not received, believed, and owned, then all other truths are useless to our hearts.
2. The light of faith is given to us to help us see the glory of God in Jesus—to meditate on it in all its ways. If we do not have this light, given to us by the power of God, we are strangers to the whole mystery of the gospel (Eph. 1:17–19, 2 Cor. 4:3-4).
3. When we see the glory of God in Jesus, we also see his glory. In this, he is infinitely glorious above all creation, because in and through him, the glory of the invisible God is represented to us. This is where our hearts are alive, when the

image of God is renewed in us, and we are made new.

4. This is necessary for Christians to carry out our spiritual duties, because someone who does not know Jesus, the Gospel, or the church, cannot hope to do so. It is the root that all Christian duties grow from, distinguishing our works from those of non-believers. Someone who does not believe that faith in Jesus is the spring of all spiritual obedience or does not know faith respects the revelation of the glory of God in him, is not a Christian!

Is It Unfamiliar?

To those who have not yet considered this mystery and how to exercise faith in it, I have these directions:

1. Know that seeing the glory of Jesus and all his holy attributes is the greatest privilege we can have in this life. A glimpse of heaven is in it, and the first taste of glory, because this is life eternal: to know the Father, and Jesus whom he sent (John 17:3). Unless you value it, unless you see it as a privilege, you will not enjoy it, and anything you do not value for its worth is despised. It is not enough to think it is a privilege or an advantage, but it is to be valued above other things for its greatness. "Destruction and Death say, 'We've heard only rumors of where wisdom can be found.'" (Job 28:22, NLT). If we do not value it, we will die as strangers to it, but if we want to gain it, we

must "call out for insight and raise [our] voice for understanding" (Prov. 2:3).

2. It is not just a great privilege, it is also a great mystery, which requires much spiritual wisdom to understand it properly (1 Cor. 2:4-5). Flesh and blood will not reveal it to us, but God must teach us to take hold of it (John 1:12-13; Matt. 16:16-17). Natural logic will never enable us or guide us to understand this duty. As much as we would like to have a skill and understanding of something, we cannot have it without putting in the hard work to get it. It is the same with spiritual skills and wisdom—we cannot gain it without diligently using the methods God has given us to attain it. The main technique is fervent prayer. So, pray, like Moses did, that God will show you his glory; pray like Paul, that "the eyes of your hearts [are] enlightened, that you may know;" and "that the God of our Lord Jesus Christ, the Father of glory, may give you the Spirit of wisdom and of revelation in the knowledge of him" (Eph. 1:17-18). Fill your mind with spiritual thoughts about them. Lazy hearts never see this glory, because the devil distracts them. Being naturally minded, they do not like prayer and meditation as it is not satisfying and difficult.

3. Learn to avoid bad habits. When our minds are focused on our lusts, that is all we think about until we "have eyes full of adultery, insatiable for sin" (2 Pet. 2:14). The objects of our lusts become fixed in our minds, transforming us into their likeness. If we are lazy and give in,

our hearts become filled with destruction, until every word, gesture, and action reveals what we long for. Should we be lazy and negligent in thinking about this glory that transforms our minds into its own likeness? Our eyes of our understanding should be continually filled with it until we see him continually, then we will never stop delighting in him and loving him.

4. We must see the glory of God as he reveals it in his attributes—without this, we have nothing of the power of Christianity in us, no matter what we pretend. Look at creation and everything in it; there is nothing more to say, but "We have heard of your fame and about all these things," and what we have heard we declare. But it is only a small portion we see and know. "The heavens declare the glory of God, and the sky above proclaims his handiwork" (Ps. 19:1). "For his invisible attributes, namely, his eternal power and divine nature, have been clearly perceived, ever since the creation of the world, in the things that have been made" (Rom. 1:20). But, there is more we can learn about them in Jesus than in creation. The greatest philosopher knew little compared to the least of the apostles in this.

Seeking His Glory

But we must not rest in the idea of this truth or a small approval of its doctrine. The power of it on our hearts is what we must aim for.

- Where do the saints in heaven find their happiness?
- Is it not in knowing and seeing the glory of God in Jesus?
- And what is the effect of this on their souls?
- Does it not change them into the same image or make them like Jesus?
- Does it fill and satisfy them with joy, rest, delight, and peace?
- Do we expect and desire the same happiness?

It is our view of Jesus' glory now that is our initiation, and if we continue, we will experience its transforming power in our souls.

Some people are still babies when it comes to spiritual knowledge and understanding because they are carnal (1 Cor. 3:1-2) or lazy in hearing (Heb. 5:12-14), and so are not capable of these divine mysteries. That is why Paul says in 1 Cor. 2:6-7, that the wisdom of God is revealed to those who are more mature in spiritual knowledge, because they "have their powers of discernment trained by constant practice to distinguish good from evil" (Heb. 5:14), think on heavenly things, and delight to walk in the ancient paths of faith and love.

He Is Glorified in Redeeming the Church

The attributes of God's nature are not only represented in Jesus but also in the power of salvation of the church. In him we see and know the wisdom, goodness, love, grace, mercy, and power of God, working to accomplish the work of our redemption and salvation. This gives an incredible brilliance to all his wonderful qualities. The wisdom and love of God are infinitely glorious—nothing can be added to them—there can be no increase of their essential glory. However, as they are eternally part of God's nature, we cannot see their full glory, except as they are revealed in the work of the redemption and salvation of the church. As they are expressed, imparting blessings to the souls of those that believe, so the rays of their glory shine down on us with unspeakable refreshment and joy (2 Cor. 4:6).

This is why Paul says:

Oh, the depth of the riches and wisdom and knowledge of God! How unsearchable are his judgments and how inscrutable his ways! "For who has known the mind of the Lord, or who has been his counselor?" "Or who has given a gift to him that he might be repaid?" For from him and through him and to him are all things. To him be glory forever. Amen. (Rom. 11:33–36)

We Believe in God Through Him

"Who through him are believers in God" (1 Pet. 1:21). This is the life of our souls. God himself, in his perfection and divine nature, is the ultimate object of our faith. On earth, we do not see him directly, but this is God's way and method of revealing himself and them to us. Through Jesus, we believe in God. By believing in him, we ultimately place our faith in God himself, and this we cannot do except by seeing the glory of God in him.

We Know God Through Him

This is the only way we can have the saving, sanctifying knowledge of God. Without this, every ray of divine light that shines on us (John 1:5), every spark that comes from the light of nature within, amazes people's minds rather than leads them to the saving knowledge of God. Just so, a glance of light on a dark night, showing a temporary view of things, and passing away, amazes a traveler instead of directing him, leaving him more exposed to going off the path than before. This is the same as all those ideas of the Divine Being and his attributes, which seemingly wise people have boasted about among unbelievers. They did change their minds but did not transform them into the image and likeness of God, as the saving knowledge of him does (Col. 3:10).

This is what Paul meant when we wrote:

Where is the one who is wise? Where is the scribe? Where is the debater of this age? Has not God made foolish the wisdom of the world? For since, in the wisdom of God, the world did not know God through wisdom, it pleased God through the folly of what we preach to save those who believe. For Jews demand signs and Greeks seek wisdom, but we preach Christ crucified, a stumbling block to Jews and folly to Gentiles, but to those who are called, both Jews and Greeks, Christ the power of God and the wisdom of God. (1 Cor. 1:20–24)

It is evident that the world, the wise, and the studious have been left by God's wisdom to themselves, in their own wisdom. But their natural light and logic cannot come to the saving knowledge of God, and instead, they are puffed up into contempt of the revelation of who he is. To them, it was weak and nonsense. So, it pleased

God to show that their wisdom was foolishness and to establish the only means of knowledge of himself in Jesus.

Study Guide - Reflections

As you work through these reflections, take your time and dwell on questions that tug at your heart, prompting you to dig a little further. God's Word is not a glorified storybook; it is life and spirit, able to cut between bone and marrow, so the issues we are unaware of or want to hide are brought to the light. This is growth—when we admit we need to grow in areas, and we need God's help to do it. We need his Holy Spirit to understand these spiritual things.

This chapter is the launchpad for the following few chapters that all build onto this concept of Jesus as God and man, fulfilling the role of mediator. It is the pouring of the foundation that must be done properly before anything can be added. As Paul himself said, "I laid a foundation, and someone else is building upon it. Let each one take care how he builds upon it" (1 Cor. 3:10). John Owen approaches this subject methodically, step by step to make sure that the correct order is followed for us to understand.

1. What is so important about Jesus' statement that those who see him have seen the Father?
2. What does wisdom and love have to do with seeing the glory of Christ?
3. What arguments does Owen have for those

who don't want to understand the things of God and his glory?
4. What does he say to those who are not against it but choose not to get involved?
5. Do you find yourself in these categories sometimes, even though you're a Christian?

3

THE GLORY OF CHRIST AS MAN AND GOD

The second way we see the glory of Jesus is in his Person: he is God and man in one. He has two distinct natures: eternal, infinite, immense, almighty—the form and essence of God; and also finite, limited, confined to a certain place—our human nature he took on when he "became flesh and dwelt among us" (John 1:14).

This is the glory that shines so bright that the blind world cannot bear the light and beauty of it. Many people openly deny this incarnation of the Son of God, this personal union of God and man. They deny that there is any glory or truth in it, and there are even more who remain quiet about not believing the truth or seeing any glory in it. However, this glory is the glory of Christianity—the glory of the church and the Rock on which it is built—the only source of present grace and future glory.

This is the glory that the angels desire to see, the "things into which [they] long to look" (1 Peter 1:12). This was even represented in the holiest place of the Tabernacle: the ark and mercy seat were a symbol of Jesus, and these cherubim stood over them, looking down in reverence and adoration.

This is the downfall of Satan and his kingdom. His sin consisted of two parts:

1. His pride against the person of the Son of God, by whom he was created. "For by him all things were created, in heaven and on earth, visible and invisible, whether thrones or dominions or rulers or authorities" (Col. 1:16). Against Jesus, he exalted himself—the beginning of his transgression.
2. Envy against mankind, made in the image of God. This completed his sin. God, in his infinite wisdom, unites both natures that Satan sinned against, into the one person of Jesus. This led to the devil's destruction and eternal shame when he realized his mistake in fighting against the powers of these two natures united in one person.

This is the foundation of the church. Creation was made through the absolute sovereign power of God who "hangs the earth on nothing" (Job 26:7). But the foundation of the church is on this mysterious, immovable rock, "You are the Christ, the Son of the living God" (Matt. 16:16). It is the most intimate combination of the two natures, the divine and human, although different, in the same person. Isaiah shows this to us:

For to us a child is born, to us a son is given; and the government shall be upon his shoulder, and his name shall be called Wonderful Counselor, Mighty God, Everlasting Father, Prince of Peace. (Isa. 9:6).

The church must fall down and worship the Author of this wonderful combination, drawn to obedience in faith, and humbly adoring what cannot be fully understood.

It was hinted at in Exodus 3:2–6:

And the angel of the Lord appeared to him in a flame of fire out of the midst of a bush. He looked, and behold, the bush was burning, yet it was not consumed. And Moses said, "I will turn aside to see this great sight, why the bush is not burned." When the Lord saw that he turned aside to see, God called to him out of the bush, "Moses, Moses!" And he said, "Here I am." Then he said, "Do not come near; take your sandals off your feet, for the place on which you are standing is holy ground." And he said, "I am the God of your father, the God of Abraham, the God of Isaac, and the God of Jacob."

This fire was a symbol of the presence of God in the person of the Son. He is called an Angel—the Angel of the covenant—but absolutely in himself, he was Jehovah, the "God of Abraham." The fire was also fitting since he is a "consuming fire" (Heb. 12:29) and his task was delivering the church out of a fiery trial. This fire burned in a bush, but the bush was not consumed, and so God was said to live in the bush: "The favor of him who dwells in the bush" (Deut. 33:16). The fire was a symbol of him in whom "the whole fullness of deity dwells bodily" forever (Col. 2:9), and of him who "became flesh and dwelt among us" (John 1:14). The eternal fire of the divine nature lives in the bush of our frail human nature, yet is it not consumed by it.

As Moses was told to take his shoes off, so we are taught to throw off all fleshly thoughts and natural desires, that by pure acts of faith, we can see this glory—the glory of the only-begotten of the Father.

Think on His Glory

We must resolve in our hearts and minds that this glory of Jesus is the best, the most noble, useful, beneficial topic we can talk and think about, or desire after.

What else can compare with "knowing Christ Jesus my Lord?" According to Paul, everything else is "rubbish" (Phil. 3:8–10). We are living in the flesh if it is not the same for us.

What is the world, and everything in it, that people think about and desire? The Psalmist answers with this comparison of seeing the glory of Christ: "Who will show us some good?"—Who can give us anything from the world that will give our minds peace and satisfaction? But, he says, "Lift up the light of your face upon us, O LORD!" (Ps. 4:6). The light of the glory of God in the face of Jesus is the only satisfying thing I desire and seek.

The Bible rebukes the arrogance and foolishness of people who "spend your money for that which is not bread, and your labor for that which does not satisfy" (Isa. 55:2). They spend all their energy on things that do not last when they have everlasting riches offered to them.

What do people think about most of the time? What fills their thoughts?

Some people focus on the "provision for the flesh, to gratify its desires" (Rom. 13:14). They are constantly searching in their minds for things to satisfy their lusts and natural desires, imprinting them into their brains. They fix their eyes on everything dirty, filthy things—sinful pleasures—refusing to look at the beauty and glory of the light of the sun—the glory of Christ.

Some only think about the things of this world to see what they can get from them, and so, are transformed into the image of the world, becoming worldly, carnal, and proud. Is it because there is no God in Israel that they turn to the idol of Ekron? Is there no glory, no desire to seek after Jesus, to fill their minds with? What blindness, darkness, and foolishness of poor sinners!

Some, who are more educated and logical, spend time meditating on the works of creation and destiny. That is why we have lots of wonderful discussions on these subjects, published in incredible writing. It appeals to our nature and our rational thinking, but there is no glory in them to compare with the mysterious person of Jesus. The sun's glory, the moon, and stars' beauty, and the wonder of celestial bodies cannot compare with him.

This is what is declared in Psalm 8:1-6:

O Lord, our Lord, how majestic is your name in all the earth! You have set your glory above the heavens. Out of the mouth of babies and infants, you have established strength because of your foes, to still the enemy and the avenger. When I look at your heavens, the work of your fingers, the moon and the stars, which you have set in place, what is man that you are mindful of him, and the son of man that you care for him? Yet you have made him a little lower than the heavenly beings and crowned him with glory and honor. You have given him dominion over the works of your hands; you have put all things under his feet.

It looks at the glory of God in his works, that heaven, with the moon and stars (which he meditated on at night), was incredibly glorious, and awesome. It then looks at the poor, weak nature of humans, which cannot compare with the glory of the heavens. Then it suddenly turns to admire the wisdom, goodness, and love of God, exalting that nature above all creation in the person of Jesus Christ, as is also reflected in Hebrews 2:5-6.

No Comparison

So, this is the highest and best thing we can set our thoughts and emotions on. Anyone who has seen this glory, even though they are just poor, sinful, dying worms of the earth, would refuse to be like an angel if it meant giving up seeing it. This is where every manifestation of the divine glory comes together.

Look at the things of this world: wives, husbands, children, possessions, land, power, friends, and honor; how pleasing and good they are! How most people long for these things! But anyone who has seen the glory of Christ, will say, "Whom have I in heaven but you? And there is nothing on earth that I desire besides you" (Ps. 73:25), "For who in the skies can be compared to the Lord? Who among the heavenly beings is like the Lord" (Ps. 89:6).

Out of his infinite love, when he looked at his church, and his blessings on it, he says "You have captivated my heart, my sister, my bride; you have captivated my heart with one glance of your eyes, with one jewel of your necklace" (Song. 4:9).

How much more should a Christian who sees the glory of Christ, to whom the Father has given everything, say, *"You have captivated my heart."* One glance at your glorious beauty has overwhelmed me—left me with no desire for earthly things. If we do not have this as our focus and desire, if we are not diligent in looking up to see his glory, it is because we are worldly and naturally minded, and do not share in the promise, that "eyes will behold the king in his beauty" (Isa. 33:17).

Study the Scriptures

The second thing we need to do is study the Bible and everything it says about the glory of Christ. We need to see it is not something made up in our minds or that others have created, but it is from faith that comes from godly revelations. This command comes from Jesus: "Search the Scriptures because… they that bear witness about me" (John 5:39). This was shown to us by the prophets in the Old Testament (1 Peter 1:11–13).

We should always hold on to this when reading the Bible—that the revelation and doctrine of the person of Jesus is the foundation that everything the prophets and apostles said about the church is built and resolved (Eph. 2:20–22). Jesus also made this clear many times in Luke 24:26, 27, 45, and 46. If we do not consider this, then the Bible is not what it should be: a revelation of the glory of God in the salvation of the church. Those who are under the law, like the Jews, cannot see this (2 Cor. 3:13–16). These revelations of the person and glory of Jesus are hidden in the Bible from the beginning to the end, revealed in faith and to Christians, even though they will not be completely understood in this life. The life of faith is mostly about meditating on these revelations.

There are three ways the glory of Jesus is shown in the Bible through:

1. descriptions of his glorious person and incarnation (Gen. 3:15, Ps. 2:7–9, Ps. 45:2–6, Ps. 69:17-18, Isa. 6:1–4, Isa. 9:6, Zech. 3:8; John 1:1–3, Phil. 2:6–8, Heb. 1:1–3, Heb. 2:14–16, Rev. 1:17-18).
2. prophecies, promises, and commands concerning him that lead us to consider his glory. There are many of these.
3. the holy practice of worship in the Old Testament, all of which was designed to

represent the glory of Christ to the church, as we will see later.

His personal appearances in the Old Testament showed his glory. We see this when Isaiah had a vision, when he saw his glory, "I saw the Lord sitting upon a throne, high and lifted up; and the train of his robe filled the temple. Above him stood the seraphim," (Isa. 6:1-2), It was a representation of the glory of Jesus, the temple of his body, with a train of all-glorious blessings. And if this was so glorious that the angels could not look, but covered their faces, then how much more glorious is it when revealed in the Gospel!

We see the same revelation in the New Testament when Peter tells us about the Mount of Transfiguration:

For when he received honor and glory from God the Father, and the voice was borne to him by the Majestic Glory, "This is my beloved Son, with whom I am well pleased," we ourselves heard this very voice borne from heaven, for we were with him on the holy mountain. (2 Pet. 1:17-18)

There were many other moments where God gave him honor and glory that everyone who believes in him should see and admire. This is not only for those who heard this testimony with their ears, but for all of us who long to see, think, and meditate on the glory of Jesus. From his throne, through speaking, miracles, and the Holy Spirit on him, God testified that Jesus was his eternal Son and gave him honor and glory.

So, when we read the Bible, we should search and look

for this, as the prophets did, if we want to become "wise unto salvation" (1 Tim. 3:5).

We should be like the trader who looked for pearls, and when he found one of great price, he sold or left everything to have it (Matt. 13:45-46). The Bible is the field, the place, the mine where we search and dig for pearls. (Prov. 2:1–5). Every truth that is good for our hearts is a pearl that enriches us, but when we meet Jesus, when we find this pearl of great price, the glory of Christ—this is what the heart of a Christian holds onto with joy.

We find food for our souls in the word of truth, we taste how gracious the Lord is, and the Bible becomes refreshing for us like a spring of living water, when we find the glory of Jesus in it. We will be in the best position when our main intention is to hold onto the Scripture against everything that distracts us or discourages us from searching it every day. This is the beauty of the Bible; it is the representation of the glory of Christ.

Meditate on His Glory

Another instruction is that once we have the knowledge of the glory of Jesus from the Bible, or through the preaching of the gospel, we must now meditate on it often.

The biggest mistake that keeps many of us so low is not doing this. We hear of these things and agree with them, but never meditate upon them. We might think it is above us, are ignorant of it, or see it as too radical. A worldly mind cannot find joy in this. The mind must be spiritual and holy, free from earthly emotions and distractions, raised above worldly things, so we can meditate on the glory of Jesus. But most people do not do this, because they will not deny their emotions and thoughts.

There are people who claim to meditate on Jesus' glory and claim to desire seeing it, but never actually make the time to do so. But it is clear that these things do not match up. It is impossible for a person who never meditates on the glory of Jesus here on earth, and who does not try and see it by faith as it is shown in the Bible, to ever have any real desire to see it in heaven. They may love and desire the idea of it, but they are ignorant and do not know the glory of Jesus. It is sad that people can find time for other things that are worldly and useless but do not have the heart or inclination to meditate on this incredible thing. What faith and love do they have? How they are deceived.

Think Often of Jesus

Think about Jesus often, every day. He is not far from us, and we can talk to him at any time. Paul tells us,

Do not say in your heart, 'Who will ascend into heaven?'" (that is, to bring Christ down) "or 'Who will descend into the abyss?'" (that is, to bring Christ up from the dead). But what does it say? "The word is near you, in your mouth and in your heart." (Rom. 10:6–8)

The things Jesus did were all in the past, but here "The word" of the Gospel where these things are revealed is near to us, even in our hearts. If we are true believers and have read the Word with faith, it will reveal Jesus and all the benefits of his mediation to us. If this word is in our hearts, Jesus is near to us. When we look at the word that is in our hearts, he is ready to commune with us. The light of the knowledge of Jesus which we have by the word will be in our minds.

To show how near he is to us, it says, he stands at the door and knocks, (Rev. 3:20). For he is always accompanied by the glorious train of his character; and if they are not received, neither is he. It does not help to boast about Christ if we do not have any evidence of his character in our hearts and lives. But if he is our hope of future glory, then he is the life of present grace in us.

Sometimes He might feel far away, so we cannot hear his voice, see his face, or feel his love, even though we seek him with diligence. In this state, all our thoughts and meditations about him will be dry and fruitless, bringing no spiritual refreshment to our souls. And if we learn to be content with such lifeless thoughts that bring no experience of his love or give us a real view of his glory, the power of Christianity will die in us.

A Desire

The spouse in the Song of Songs represents the heart we as believers should have if we want to experience these things:

On my bed by night I sought him whom my soul loves; I sought him, but found him not. I will rise now and go about the city, in the streets and in the squares; I will seek him whom my soul loves. I sought him, but found him not. The watchmen found me as they went about in the city. "Have you seen him whom my soul loves?" Scarcely had I passed them when I found him whom my soul loves. (Song. 3:1–4)

This is an example of the desire we should have. Jesus can sometimes withdraw himself from the spiritual experience of believers, so there is no refreshing sense of his love, or his fresh mercy and grace. Those who have never experienced refreshing communion with him would not realize when it is absent—they never knew his presence to realize it was gone. But those he has visited and given his love, made his home, refreshed, relieved, and comforted, and lived in the power of his grace—they know what it is to be forsaken by him, even if it just for a moment. They become desperate when they diligently seek to find his presence and cannot find him. Our duty is to persevere in prayer, meditation, reading, and hearing of the Word, in all personal and corporate worship, until we find him, or he returns to us.

A Diligence

It would be good if all churches and Christians had the same diligence as the early church had. But many do not have the same heart as this spouse because they are lazy, careless, negligent, and do not motivate themselves to search for him. This is how it was in Laodicea and Sardis, and many Christians today.

Jesus is near and accessible to every believer, and the life of faith consists in how often we think on him because this is how Jesus lives in us (Gal. 2:20). We cannot do this unless we frequently think of him and converse with him, then he lives in us. He lives in us by faith.

If we want to see the glory of Jesus, then we must think on it. I am not talking about meditating or having quiet times, but about fleeting thoughts throughout the day. It is a detriment to us if we have not thought about Jesus for a long time. Thinking about him is one of the best characteristics of a truly spiritual Christian.

Have an Attitude of Worship

All our thoughts about Jesus and his glory should be filled with admiration, adoration, and thanksgiving. If we are spiritually renewed, our senses are focused on this glorious object. This is why we are commanded to "love the Lord your God with all your heart and with all your soul and with all your mind and with all your strength" (Mark 12:30). Everything in us should be absorbed by God's love. In heaven, when we are in complete peace, we will only be focused on one infinite, invariable object of our minds and emotions, without any interruption. But while we are on earth, we only see a part of it and need to engage in faith and love to view that glory. Through grace, we admire, adore, and thank the glory that we are able to see because this sustains us.

On Judgment Day, he will be "marveled at among all who have believed" (2 Thess. 1:10). Even Christians will be overwhelmed with awe at his glorious appearance, because of his grace and power in their redemption, sanctification, resurrection, and glory. We should marvel since we will be part of that glory.

And this admiration will bring adoration and thanksgiving as we see in the example of the renewed church.

And they sang a new song, saying, "Worthy are you to take the scroll and to open its seals, for you were slain, and by your blood you ransomed people for God from every tribe and language and people and nation, and you have made them a kingdom and priests to our God, and they shall reign on the earth." Then I looked, and I heard around the throne and the living creatures and the elders the voice of many angels, numbering myriads of myriads and thousands of thousands, saying with a loud voice, "Worthy is the Lamb who was slain, to receive power and wealth and wisdom and might and honor and glory and blessing!" And I heard every creature in heaven and on earth and under the earth and in the sea, and all that is in them, saying, "To him who sits on the throne and to the Lamb be blessing and honor and glory and might forever and ever!" And the four living creatures said, "Amen!" and the elders fell down and worshiped. (Rev. 5:9–14)

The glory of Christ should not just be an idea of truth we agree with, but something we allow to affect our hearts so that we may be changed into his image.

People's minds are worldly, unable to discern spiritual things—they despise them because they do not understand them. These ancient paths are not for those people. They cannot sit at the feet of Jesus with Mary when she chooses the better part, because they are like Martha, distracted by many things of the world. Their only goal is to satisfy themselves now and satisfy their lusts. They can think about everything except the things that are above; those do not concern them.

Others claim they want to see the glory of Jesus by faith, but it is too spiritual and difficult for them. They become overwhelmed when they see it. They are like the disciples who saw him in his transfiguration—they were filled with amazement, and do not know what to say.

Study Guide - Reflections

Christianity is not the only religion to recognize Jesus as a key figure in spirituality. Islam, Judaism, and many others are quick to extol his virtues, even including some of his teachings in their sacred texts. But they stop short when it comes to admitting he was not just a man but also God. We see him in his full capacity in this incredible and impossible dual role: both man and God at the same time! He is not just a part of Christianity; he is the very center of it all.

When we begin to see this and embrace him as our Lord, God, and Savior, we are on the right track to seeing his glory manifest in our lives. As we have read, Satan will do everything in his power to break, obscure, or confuse this picture of Jesus, dumbing him down to a good man, a friendly guru, or one of the gods! If he can remove him from his throne in our minds, he has effectively denied us the blessing and benefit of a full spiritual life. And unfortunately, many Christians have fallen into this trap of not seeing Jesus for who he is.

1. Why is it important to see that Jesus was both God and man at the same time?
2. Do you personally relate to Jesus more as man or more as God? Why?
3. Thinking about Jesus, reading the Bible, and meditating on him are the three ways Owen says we can increase our faith to see his glory. Which of these do you struggle with the most?
4. Are you able to say those words without any doubt or hesitation: "*You have captivated my heart*"?
5. Owen speaks about being diligent in thinking about Jesus and reading the Bible. Are you diligent, disciplined, and determined in these areas?

4

THE GLORY OF CHRIST AS MEDIATOR

Everything discussed so far may not be easy to understand, especially if you are not aware of spiritual matters. But these can become clearer if you are willing to learn. The following is not as easy to understand, dealing with the glory of Christ as mediator.

Seeing the glory of Jesus as mediator should be one of our main goals of faith:

I count everything as loss because of the surpassing worth of knowing Christ Jesus my Lord... that I may know him and the power of his resurrection, and may share his sufferings, becoming like him in his death. (Phil. 3:8,10)

"For there is one God," Paul says, "and there is one mediator between God and men, the man Christ Jesus" (1 Tim. 2:5). The rift between God and man was brought on by our sin that leads to the destruction of all humans, and there was no one in heaven or earth who was able to restore righteous peace between them. For this, there must be a mediator.

God could not do it himself because "an intermediary implies more than one, but God is one" (Gal. 3:20). Despite his sovereign grace, he could not mediate. And there are no people who can fill this role because "If someone sins against a man, God will mediate for him, but if someone sins against the Lord, who can intercede for him?" (1 Sam. 2:25). "There is no arbiter between us, who might lay his hand on us both" (Job 9:33).

Jesus, as the Son of God, said, "Sacrifices and offerings you have not desired, but a body have you prepared for me… I have come to do your will" (Heb. 10:5, 9). In taking on human form, and as God, he fulfilled this role and continues to do so.

When it comes to the glory of Jesus as mediator, there are three things to consider:

1. taking on the role of mediator
2. fulfilling it
3. the consequence of him doing so

In becoming mediator, we can see the glory of Jesus as he assumed this role, revealing his humility and love. When Jesus did this, it was in godly condescension (stepping down from heaven, taking a position lower than himself). This was not by chance or forced on him against his will. He had no need of it for himself, but willingly stepped down and condescended to assume the role.

So, Paul said,

> Have this mind among yourselves, which is yours in Christ Jesus, who, though he was in the form of God, did not count equality with God a thing to be grasped, but emptied himself, by taking the form of a servant, being born in the likeness of men. And being found in human form, he humbled himself by becoming obedient to the point of death, even death on a cross. (Phil. 2:5–8)

Jesus' attitude in this is what we must notice—he was prepared to do it. He emptied himself. His condescension was an act of humbling himself (Ps. 113:6). Becoming human in order to fill the role of mediator was an infinite condescension of the Son of God, and as Christians, we can see his glory in the following:

1. the greatness of his condescension
2. the special nature of it
3. the view of the glory of Christ in this

The Greatness of Jesus as Mediator

God's divine nature is so incredible that he is described as "seated on high," and as one who "looks far down on the heavens and the earth" (Ps. 113:5-6). He condescends from his exalted place above to look and notice the most glorious things in heaven above and on the earth below. When he pays attention to his creation or creatures, it is an act of infinite condescension.

First, it is because of the infinite distance between who he is and his creation. To him, all nations "are like a drop from a bucket, and are accounted as the dust on the scales," and "are as nothing before him, they are accounted by him as less than nothing and emptiness" (Isa. 40:15, 17). That is why God's infinite distance from the nature of all creatures requires him to condescend, step down, or humble himself.

For thus says the One who is high and lifted up, who inhabits eternity, whose name is Holy: "I dwell in the high and holy place, and also with him who is of a contrite and lowly spirit, to revive the spirit of the lowly, and to revive the heart of the contrite." (Isa. 57:15)

He is so exalted, living in his own eternal being, that it is his grace to take notice of things below, especially those the world despises.

Secondly, it comes from his infinite self-sufficiency. Everything we need and want is for our own satisfaction; no creature is self-sufficient. The human nature of Jesus lives in God, and God in it, fully dependent on God. It is only God who does not need or want anything. Nothing can be added to him since he "gives to all mankind life and breath and everything" (Acts 17:25). All creation cannot add one bit to the satisfaction or wonder of God,;he has everything in infinite perfection in himself.

He does not benefit from our goodness or our works as another person would.

If you have sinned, what do you accomplish against him? And if your transgressions are multiplied, what do you do to him? If you are righteous, what do you give to him? Or what does he receive from your hand? (Job 35:6-7)

So, all God's attention on creation is simply him stooping down from his exalted place—condescension.

Therefore, the Son of God's condescension to fill the role of mediator is incredible! Because of the perfection of his godly nature, his infinite distance from creation, and his self-sufficiency, what heart can understand or mouth explain the glory of the condescension of Jesus as he took our nature upon him in order to mediate on our behalf?

The Special Nature of His Mediation

Non-Biblical Myths

In looking at the special nature of what Jesus did, we must debunk the myths about it and declare the truth.

He Did Not Leave His Godly Nature

Jesus did not lay aside, leave, or separate from his nature so that he stopped being God to become man. He was "he was in the form of God, did not count equality with God a thing to be grasped" (Phil. 2:6). He was completely God: he declared himself equal with God the Father. He was in the form of God: he was God in nature, equal with God in authority, dignity, and power. Because he was in the form of God, he must be equal with God, because there is order in the Trinity, but no inequality. So, the Jews understood him, when he was "calling God his own Father, making himself equal with God." By saying this, he gave himself equal power with the Father in every way. "My Father is working until now, and I am working" (John 5:17-18).

He took on him the form of a servant (Phil. 2:7). This is his condescension. He did not stop being God but also became what he was not. Jesus said, "No one has ascended into heaven except he who descended from heaven, the Son of Man" (John 3:13). Although he was on earth as the Son of man, he did not stop being God —in his divine nature, he was also in heaven.

Someone who is God cannot stop being God, the same way someone who is not God can be God. We believe that Jesus, being God, was made human for our sake, not that he was a man made into a god!

This condescension is the foundation of the glory of Jesus, the life and soul of all godly truth and mysteries: the Son of God stepping down in time to be what he was not, the Son of man, yet still remained what he was, the eternal Son of God.

He Did Not Transform His Godly Nature

This condescension also was not the conversion of godly nature into human. Some argue that the Word which was in the beginning, turned into flesh, the same way Jesus turned water into wine—it stopped being water and was completely wine, not water mixed with wine (John 1:1). But there is no glory in this false condescension of Jesus. It destroys both his natures and leaves him as a person in whom we are not concerned.

He Did Not Change His Godly Nature

This condescension did not result in the smallest change or alteration in his divine nature. Some believed he had two natures—the divine and human combined into one. And this could not happen without affecting the divine nature. But, even though Jesus became what he was not before, in that he took on our humanity, his godly nature was not human. In God, there is "no variation or shadow due to change" (James 1:17). In every way, as it was from eternity, so it was in Jesus, without changing or losing anything of his godly nature. Jesus suffered through many things as a human in life and death, but his divine nature never did—however, going through it all, he was still God, and so he "obtained with his own blood" (Acts 20:28).

He Was Not Just a Prophet

What did Jesus do in his godly nature in this condescension? Paul says he "emptied himself... humbled himself" (Phil. 2:7-8). He hid the glory of his divine nature in ours, so there was no physical evidence of it. The world did not see him as the true God and thought he was evil. They saw nothing of his divine nature because they looked at him with human eyes—as a man, he was no different to them. So, when he said, "Before Abraham was, I am," which is a claim of existing in another eternal nature they could not see, they were filled with rage, and "took up stones to throw at him," (John 8:58-59). The reason for their anger was "because you, being a man, make yourself God" (John 10:33). No wise and sober person could ever say something like this—claiming he was God. They could not comprehend this, because there was nothing to compare with, no person could be both God and man.

But this issue is solved by the glory of Jesus in his condescension: he was "God over all, blessed forever," yet he humbled himself for the salvation of the church, to the eternal glory of God, to take our nature upon him, to be made human (Rom. 9:5). Those who cannot see divine glory in him doing this, do not know, love, or believe in him, nor do they belong to him.

Because they cannot see the glory in this, they deny the foundation of Christianity—the divine person of Jesus. As a man, they see him as no more than a man and reject the glory of God, his infinite wisdom, goodness, and grace. They dig up the root of all evangelical truths.

Jesus Christ is "a stone of stumbling, and a rock of offense" to the world (1 Pet. 2:8). If we see him only as a prophet, a man sent by God, there would not be much contest or opposition to him. The Muslims acknowledge this, and the Jews do not deny it. Their hatred for him was, and is, because he claimed to be God. If you take this away, Christianity disappears because that is the mystery, the glory, the truth, and the value of it. This is the rock on which the church is built, against which the gates of hell will not prevail.

His Presence Was No Illusion

This condescension of Jesus was not an apparition or spiritual appearance. One of the first heresies against the early church was that everything Jesus did or suffered as a man was not that of a human, but a representation, like angels in the Old Testament appearing in the form of men, eating and drinking. So, they claimed it was an appearance of Christ in the man Jesus, in whom he suffered no more than in other believers. But these people invented an imaginary Christ, so then their salvation is also imaginary.

Biblical Truths

The true nature of this divine condescension consists of three things:

He Was Fully God and Man

The eternal person of the Son of God, through his divine power and love, assumed our nature to be his own, even as the divine nature is his. This is the foundation of faith, even to those who cannot understand all these divine mysteries. They believe that the Son of God took our nature as his own so that whatever he did was done by him, just like every other man. Every person has an individual human nature, so they are themselves and not someone else. That human nature that is common to us all becomes their own as if only they had it. Adam, the first human, was no more of an individual man than the rest of us. So, Christ taking on that nature common to us all into an individual person became the man, Jesus. This was the mind that was in him.

He Acted in His Human Nature

Because he assumed our nature, everything he did and suffered was as a man: the glory of his divine person was hidden, and he made himself of no reputation. This is his condescension.

He Experienced Our Nature

In assuming our nature to be his own, he did not change it into something divine and spiritual but kept it as it was. It really suffered, was tried, tempted, and forsaken, as any other person might be. That nature was exposed to all temptation and evil as we are (Phil. 2:5–8).

The Glory of Jesus in His Mediation

This is how we are to see the glory of Christ by faith while we are on earth.

Even if we could speak as angels, we would not be able to fully express the glory of this condescension because it is the most incredible act of the Father's wisdom and the Son's love—the greatest evidence of God's care toward mankind. Is there anything that can match it or be like it? It is the glory of Christianity and the heart of evangelical truth. The mystery of the wisdom of God is beyond the logic or understanding of men and angels; it can only be the object of our faith and admiration (Job 11:7–9, Rom. 11:33–36).

He who was eternally in the form of God—equal with God the Father—takes on the nature of man so that he was no less a man in time than he was God from eternity. Not only that, but he "emptied himself," having no reputation in this world—saying he was a worm and not a person to compare with those of any esteem.

We speak of these things humbly, we teach them as they are in the Bible, we strive by faith to follow them; but when we have a clear view and understanding of it, our minds fail, our hearts tremble, and there is no peace except in a holy admiration of what we cannot comprehend. We cannot fully grasp it while on this earth, but all the fruits and blessings of this truth are given to us who believe.

This is the promise about him for the church, that "he will become a sanctuary" (Isa. 8:14). But he will become a "stone of stumbling, and a rock of offense" to those who do not believe (1 Peter 2:7-8).

Jesus, Our Sanctuary

In this, he is a sanctuary, a refuge for all that come to him. What do we look for in a sanctuary? A provision for all our needs, a deliverance from all our fears, a defense against all our dangers. This is what Jesus is to sin-distressed souls; he is a refuge for us in all spiritual sickness and despair (Heb. 6:18). Are we burdened with sin, troubled with temptations, oppressed by a spiritual enemy, or do we walk "in darkness and *[have]* no light" (Isa. 50:10)? One view of the glory of Jesus is enough to support and relieve us.

The one who emptied and humbled himself, who stepped down from his glory and self-sufficiency, taking on our nature to become a mediator on our behalf—will he not relieve us in all our troubles? Will he not do everything for us that we need, that we may be eternally saved? Will he not be a sanctuary for us? There is no reason to believe he is powerless because in his condescension to be a suffering man, he lost no power as God omnipotent—he lost no infinite wisdom or glorious grace. He could still do all that he could do as God from eternity. The combination of infinite power and infinite condescension is all in Jesus as a sanctuary for sinners. If we see no glory in this, it is because there is no light of faith in us.

He is "a hiding place from the wind, a shelter from the storm, like streams of water in a dry place, like the shade of a great rock in a weary land" (Isa. 32:2). He says, "I will satisfy the weary soul, and every languishing soul I will replenish" (Jer. 31:25).

Jesus, a Rock of Offense

He is "a stone of offense and a rock of stumbling" to the unbelieving and disobedient, who "disobey the word." They cannot, they will not see the glory of this condescension; they hate it and despise it, allowing him no glory. They say he was just a man and no more—this was his glory. They see no glory, relief, refuge, or refreshment for their souls in this, so they deny his divine person. But faith triumphs over them as Jesus becomes a glorious sanctuary that they cannot understand.

Contemplating Him

The main act of faith is in the divine person of Christ, as all Christians must acknowledge. We do not have this if we do not see his glory in this condescension. The main duty of our obedience is self-denial, with readiness for the cross. The condescension of Christ is our example, where we learn obedience as Paul declares (Phil. 2:5–8). No one can deny themselves properly unless it is based on the self-denial of the Son of God. What do we deny? Everything we have. Our freedom, our relationships—our lives. What are all these except things that will perish? If this is a struggle for us to do in our minds and will, one look by faith of the glory of Jesus in this condescension, and what he left behind when he "emptied himself" will cure us of this selfish attitude.

Only by faith can we see the glory of Jesus as we will physically do one day in eternity. If we see no glory in it, if there is nothing of eternal admiration in it, we walk in darkness. Where are our hearts and minds, if we can see no glory in it? Thinking about it can be overwhelming and leave us with no real idea, but I desire this state of mind every day because when faith does not rest on understanding when it is too great and glorious to comprehend, we are filled with holy admiration, humble adoration, and joyful thanksgiving. This fills our hearts with "joy that is inexpressible and filled with glory" (1 Pet. 1:8).

Study Guide - Reflections

We don't usually equate glory with condescension. Stepping down and becoming less is not worthy of accolades or praise. According to the world's standards, it is the opposite and is deemed a failure! We can quickly overlook Jesus in a manger and skip to the highlight of his teaching, miracles, and death on the cross. But this act of taking on the nature of something lower than himself (and still retaining his original nature as God) is something that our minds struggle to understand. Owen even touches on how some people explain it away or simply ignore it.

However, he sees it as a key aspect of Jesus' glory and wants us to recognize the importance of what took place in the stable in Bethlehem. There's a reason the angels filled the sky to sing of his glory. It was humility and love at its most wonderful: God becoming man to take his place. All of this is corroborated in the Bible, written down to instruct and enlighten us about this incredible act. Take time to read through the verses that Owen quotes, highlighting the nature Jesus assumed and the reason he did it.

1. Why did God go through the trouble of sending Jesus to be one of us when he could have just clicked his fingers instead?
2. How does condescension fit into his plan for salvation? Read Philippians 2:6-8, Matthew 20:28.
3. Why is this concept of Jesus as both God and man such a critical but difficult one to grasp?
4. Why is Jesus' condescension an example for us? What does he expect of us? Read John 3:30, Ephesians 6:7, Matthew 20:26.
5. Do you see any glory in serving others?

5

THE GLORY OF CHRIST IN HIS LOVE

The Bible is clear on the Son of God taking on and carrying out his role as mediator.

His love is the only reason for him doing this (Gal. 2:20, 1 John 3:16, Rev. 1:5).

This is why he is glorious in a way we cannot understand—the glory of holy love is what makes his glory shine bright. There is no fear or worry in it—nothing but what is kindness and infinitely refreshing. Now that we see the glory of Jesus this way by faith, we can look at its nature.

Love of the Father

The reason Jesus took on this role of the redemption and salvation of the church, is the love of the Father. This love was there "before the foundation of the world" (Eph. 1:4), and afterward when he sent his Son to earth to do his will (John 3:16). He chose those who would be drawn to himself, through the blood of Jesus, and the sanctification of the Spirit (2 Thess. 2:13, 16; Eph. 1:4–9, 1 Peter 1:2).

This eternal act of the will of God the Father does not contain an actual acceptance and complacency in the state and condition of those who are chosen. It only plans for them on the account that they will be accepted and approved.

1. **It is God's character.** It is an act suited to his glorious nature of love, because "God is love" (1 John 4:8-9). So, the first product of God's character is communicative love. Choosing us was an eternal act of the will of God that has no other reason than what is in him—if we could look at all his attributes, we would find none more fitting to describe this action than love.
2. **It is free and undeserved.** Whatever good is done is an act of love, not dependent on us. It is the same with God choosing us. There is nothing in us to persuade the will of God to choose us because anything good in us is because of his love (Eph. 1:4).
3. **It results in love.** The fruits or effects of it are inconceivable acts of love. The many acts of love are its power (John 3:16, Jer. 31:3, Eph. 1:3–5, 1 John 4:8-9, 16).

Love of the Son

This is the eternal spring of the church through the mediation of Jesus—the love of the Son that put the Father's love into action and accomplished it.

1. **In his image.** Everyone was made in the image of God, in a state of love with him. Everything they had, have, and hope for are effects of his goodness and love. Their souls find life in loving God, preparing them for an eternal life of love in heaven.
2. **Fallen in sin.** From this state they fell from God in sin, the origin of all their miseries now and to come.
3. **Redeemable.** Despite this catastrophe, their nature was redeemable to once again enjoy God's presence.
4. **Compassion on us.** Mercy and compassion were Jesus' first acts of love toward us. A creature made in the image of God, fallen into misery, yet capable of recovery, is the true reason for God's compassion—his divine love to us in our state of distress and misery. The Bible is filled with scriptures on this (Heb. 2:14–16, Isa. 63:9). But for those who cannot be saved, there is no compassion, just as Jesus had no mercy on the fallen angels because of their nature.
5. **His delight.** Jesus had pity and compassion when he saw us in our misery, but knowing we were redeemable, his love works in and by joy. It was his delight to deliver mankind to the

glory of God (Prov. 8:30-31).
6. **From love.** Where did this compassion and delight come from, considering he is self-sufficient? Why was he so deeply concerned with us when we were lost? It is from the infinite love and goodness of his own nature and not from anything of us (Tit. 3:5).
7. **Prepared to suffer.** Jesus' willingness to take his place came from love and compassion, even though it would be very difficult for him as a person. For God, nothing is difficult, but having the nature of a man, he would have to suffer to accomplish this redemption. All his pity and mercy would be for us so that he would have none for himself—to save us when his own soul was burdened to death—that he should relieve us from our hardships by suffering the same things that we should have done. But he was not deterred from this act of love and mercy for us, for his love grew from it like a mighty stream against everything that came against it. This is why he said, "I have come to do your will, O God," it is my delight to do it (Heb. 10:5-7, Isa. 50:5-7).
8. **Became human.** Ready with this attitude of godly love, he assumed the role of mediation to redeem us in a physical body that was prepared for him. As a human, he would make this love real through his actions and words. This was the reason for him being human, filled with all grace and love for mankind. It was an instrument to show his eternal love in everything he did.

9. **Godly and human love.** This glorious love of Jesus does not only consist of his godly nature. He revealed this love when he was a man, not only God. In none of those eternal acts of love could the human nature of Christ have any interest or concern; yet it is the love of the man Christ Jesus celebrated in the Scripture.
10. **Loved us completely.** The love of Jesus is evident in his two different natures, each with their own properties, yet they are all acts of the same person. Whether it is of the eternal divine nature of the Son of God or of his human nature in time, it is still the love of Jesus. It was an act of inexpressible love in him, that he took on our nature (Heb. 2:14, 17). But it was only an act in and of his divine nature because it was decided before the existence of his human nature. In laying down his life for us, he performed an act of inconceivable love (1 John 3:16)—an act of his human nature when he offered himself and died. But both were acts of his divine person because it says that God laid down his life for us and purchased the church with his own blood.

This love of Jesus is why he is glorious, and how we see his glory. The saints in heaven have their victory in seeing this glory of Christ—their thankful contemplation of its fruits (Rev. 5:9-10).

The brightness of this glory shines in heaven with all-satisfying pleasure for the saints who see his glory. This is where knowledge passes understanding because then we see it in its fullness. But here on earth, if we are not lazy and naturally minded, we can still be refreshed with glimpses of it. When we do not understand, our admiration takes over.

Contemplating His Love

This is how we can exercise ourselves to see more of his glory:

First, train your mind to think more about heavenly things. If it is carnal, sensual, or filled with earthly things, this love of Jesus and its glory will not live in you. Sensual, worldly thoughts and meditating on the glory of the love of Jesus are totally opposed. A spirit consumed with many thoughts about normal life is an obstacle to communion with Jesus.

There are not many minds trained in this way. The deeds and words are evidence of what is in the heart. Their thoughts go all over the place, led by their emotions, and it is useless to expect them to meditate and think about the glory of Jesus in his love. A holy attitude is what is needed: following spiritual principles, looking for refreshment in heavenly things, immersing the soul in its fountain, and constantly looking for this divine glory.

Secondly, do not be satisfied with simple, shallow ideas about the love of Jesus, which do not bring glory but only deceive the mind. Everyone who believes his divine person declares his love. Anyone who thinks otherwise is not Christian, only having superficial views of it, not really knowing what it is.

To keep us from falling into this trap, we must know:

1. **Whose love it is**: The divine person of the Son of God. He is called God because of this love, so we can always identify it; "By this we know [God's] love, that he laid down his life for us" (1 John 3:16).
2. **How this wonderful love shows itself**: This love can be seen in divine nature by eternal wisdom, goodness, and grace; and in human nature by temporary acts of pity or compassion, suffering for us (Eph. 3:19, Heb. 2:14-15, Rev. 1:5).
3. **The freedom and blessing in it**: We did not deserve it at all (1 John 4:10). It was hatred, not love, that we deserved, which is why we should remain humble—the best place to see the glory of Christ.
4. **What it produces**: The power and fruit we see as a result. When we admire these things, our soul can walk in this paradise of God, and gather here and there a heavenly flower, enjoying the sweet savor of the love of Jesus (Song. 2:2–4).

We must not be content with the right ideas of the love of Jesus, but rather taste it in our hearts—the same way we can see a rich feast but eat nothing from the table. This is the spiritual attitude we must have in our minds. We must taste and see that the Lord is gracious, and that, if it does not satisfy our hearts, it will not last long in our minds. Jesus is the meat, bread, and food of our souls. There is nothing more spiritually nourishing than his love, which we should always desire.

Study Guide - Reflections

Our concept of love is very skewed because of our own human emotions and our lack of spiritual understanding. We equate love with anything from ice cream to whirlwind romances and wonder why we don't always feel goosebumps in church for Jesus. But his love is far above mere emotional affection, it is deeply ingrained in sacrifice and self-denial—two aspects that are not usually part of our earthly relationships.

His glory is not just in the fact that he loves us but in the way he showed it to us: coming to earth as a man and leaving heaven, being crucified for our sins, bearing our punishment, and taking our place. This is something that is far higher than feelings.

It is important to grasp this view of love if we want to have a clear view of his glory. We will only be able to do this when we fully understand what he gave up for us, what he did for us, and what he is busy doing. When we see the love that motivates him to go through death and suffering for us, then our perspective of his glory will become brighter.

1. What does Owen mean when he says that love is God's character?
2. Is love the first word you think of when it comes to God or does your view of him lean more toward judge, miracle worker, creator, or other names? Do you describe him as loving or angry, busy, and distant?

3. Why is it hard for us to accept God's undeserved love?
4. Why is it so important to realize that "he first loved us," and not the other way around? (1 John 4:19).
5. What are the four things we can do to keep from falling into the trap of being superficial in thinking about Jesus' love?

6

THE GLORY OF CHRIST IN HIS WORK

Jesus was glorious in assuming his role and in the way he carried it out. An invisible glory accompanied him in everything he did, in everything he suffered. It was invisible to the eyes of the world, but not God's. If people had seen it, they would not have crucified Jesus. However, it was revealed to some people, and they testified that they "have seen his glory, glory as of the only Son from the Father" (John 1:14), while others could see no "beauty that we should desire him" (Isa. 53:2). It is the same today.

We will first look at what he did in obedience, and then at how he suffered in carrying out his work.

His Obedience

It Was His Will

Jesus' obedience to God, as he said, "I delight to do your will, O my God; your law is within my heart" *(Ps.*

40:8), was no one else's choice but his. It is our duty to find this freedom, willingness, and cheerfulness in our obedience. Obedience comes from our will. The measure of our will toward God is how much obedience we will have, no more. However, before we act based on our own will, we feel obligated to obey God. Our natures are first subject to God's law, and then we voluntarily comply with those commands, but for Jesus, it was not like that. It was his will and choice to obey before he was obliged to do so. He obeyed because he wanted to before he had to. He said, "I delight to do your will, O my God," before he was obliged to do that will. By his own choice, and in his condescension and love, he was "born of a woman," and through that, "born under the law" (Gal. 4:4). In his divine person he was Lord of the law—above it—not under its commands or its curse. Even when he was a man, he was not under its curse because he was innocent, but also because he was above the law itself.

This was the original glory of his obedience. The wisdom, grace, love, and coming to earth that was in this choice, all of which gave life and energy to his actions and obedience—that made it pleasing to God, and useful for us. So, when he went to John to be baptized, even though he did not need it and could have declined, replied, "Let it be so now, for thus it is fitting for us to fulfill all righteousness" (Matt. 3:15). I have done this willingly, of my own accord, without any need of it for myself, and so I will do it. For Jesus, Lord of all, to submit himself to obedience is evidence of glorious grace.

It Was Selfless

This obedience was not for himself but for us. It was required of us, but we could not do it—it was not required of him, but a free act of his own will, and he did it. God gave him this honor: that he should obey for the whole churchso that by "his obedience many should be made righteous" (Rom. 5:19). God gave him honor and glory so his obedience would become the perfect obedience of the church for justification.

It Was Perfect

His obedience was complete and perfect: a representation of the holiness of God in the law. It was glorious when the finger of God wrote the Ten Commandments on stone, but even more so when they are spiritually written on our hearts as believers. But obedience is only complete and perfect in the holiness and obedience of Jesus.

It Was a Suffering

He performed this obedience through many hardships and oppositions. He was completely free from the sin that invaded our natures, making obedience difficult, and perfect obedience impossible for us. However, the opposition, temptations, sufferings, and rebukes he faced were more than any of us have encountered. This is why it says, "Although he was a son, he learned obedience through what he suffered" (Heb. 5:8).

It Was Surrender

The glory of this obedience came from the person who surrendered to God. It was the Son of God who had become man—God and man in one person. The one in heaven, above all, Lord of all, at the same time, lived in the world with no reputation but was strictly obedient to God's law. The one who receives prayer also prayed every night and day. The one who every angel of heaven and every creature worshiped also fulfilled his duties in worshiping God. The one in charge of the house served in the lowest role of the house. The one who made all men, in whose hands they are like clay in the potter's hand, observed the rules of justice. This is the obedience of Jesus that is both mysterious and glorious.

His Suffering

The glory of Christ is also revealed in his suffering as he followed God's will. He was assured victory and success with great glory (Isa. 63:1–5), but he was also required to suffer, which is why it says, "Was it not necessary that the Christ should suffer these things and enter into his glory?" (Luke 24:26).

But these sufferings of Jesus are too great for us to understand or imagine them properly. Anyone who launched into this ocean quickly found themselves unable to fathom the depths of it. Instead of trying to explain them, which I cannot, I will only point out its link to glory.

We might see Jesus under the wrath of God and the curse of the law, taking on all judgment that God ever threatened to sin or sinners. We might see his agony and bloody sweat, his strong cries and prayers, when he was near death, and we will be amazed at the terrible trial he was entering into. We might see him opposing the powers of darkness, the rage and madness of men— suffering in his soul, body, name, reputation, and life.

Some of these came straight from God, and others from demons or evil men acting according to God's will. We might see him praying, weeping, crying out, bleeding, dying—making his soul an offering for sin. "By oppression and judgment he was taken away; and as for his generation, who considered that he was cut off out of the land of the living, stricken for the transgression of my people?" (Isa. 53:8). But I will not look at these now.

Lord, what is man, that you think of him, the son of man, that you visit him? Who has known your mind or been your counselor? Oh, the rich depth of the wisdom and knowledge of God, how unsearchable are his judgments and his ways! What can we say about these things? That God did not spare his only Son but gave over to death, and all the evil in it, for the poor, lost sinners that we were—for our sake, the eternal Son of God submitted himself to every evil our natures opposed, and our sins deserved, that we might be delivered!

How glorious is Jesus in the eyes of believers! When Adam sinned, eternally ruining himself and all his descendants, he stood ashamed, afraid, trembling, ready to perish forever under God's displeasure. He deserved death and looked for it.

In this state, Jesus comes to him in a promise and says,

Poor creature! how terrible is your condition and your appearance! What has become of the beauty and glory of that image of God you were created in? How you have taken on the form and image of Satan. And yet your present misery cannot compare with what is to come. Eternal damnation lies at the door. But look up once more, and see me, that you might catch a glimpse of the infinite wisdom, love, and grace in my plans. Come out of your hiding, and I will take your place. I will take on the burden of guilt and punishment that wants to drown you eternally into hell. I will pay what I do not owe, and be made a curse for you, that you might find eternal favor.

This is how Jesus is shown in the Gospel, "publicly portrayed as crucified" before our eyes (Gal. 3:1)—the representation that is made of his glory—in the suffering he went through. Let us see him poor, despised, persecuted, reproached, nailed to a tree—under the judgment of God for our sins. But what is the glory in these things? Are these not the same things that caused the Jews and Gentiles to stumble, and that they took offense at? Was it not foolish to look for help and deliverance in the suffering of someone else—to look for life through his death as Paul mentions (1 Cor. 1)? But even in these things he is honorable, glorious, and precious to those who believe (1 Pet. 2:6-7). For even there, he was "the power of God and the wisdom of God" (1 Cor. 1:24). Paul goes on to discuss the different thoughts and apprehensions of people concerning the cross and sufferings of Jesus (2 Cor. 4:3-6).

Study Guide - Reflections

The glory Jesus has in his work as a mediator is often not fully understood. We either ignore it and focus on his position as God, king, or teacher, which is easier for our minds to get around. Or perhaps we see him as some kind of middle-man, go-between, or negotiator who is not totally necessary but helps things go smoother! As a result, we do not see much of his glory. We cannot praise him in his fullness since we do not realize what he has done and continues to do for us.

This role of mediator is critical because all salvation, reconciliation, and justification hinge on it. Without it, the yawning chasm of sin that separates us from God remains an insurmountable barrier. We are cut off and God will not, cannot accept us, no matter how good we are and how hard we try. But Jesus stepped in as the necessary sacrifice and advocate. He died in our place, paid the ransom, and now continues by interceding on our behalf. He deserves the glory for his work.

1. What new aspect of Jesus' mediation and intervention did you learn about in this chapter? Does it change your view of him?
2. What do you understand by the word mediator and why was it vital?
3. Why is it so important that there is only *one* mediator? See 1 Timothy 2:3-6.
4. Why is love such a major part of this whole plan? What does that mean for you?
5. Toward the end of this chapter, Owen lists different ways we can train and exercise ourselves to see the glory of Jesus. What are they and which ones do you need to work on in your own life?

7

THE GLORY OF CHRIST IN EXALTATION

Next, we see the glory of Jesus in God's attitude and action toward him as he carried out his mission on earth, resulting in his own exaltation.

All the prophecies and predictions concerning Jesus in the Old Testament point to two things: "the sufferings of Christ and the subsequent glories" (1 Peter 1:11). So, when he revealed it to his disciples, he explained the full doctrine there: "Was it not necessary that the Christ should suffer these things and enter into his glory?" (Luke 24:26). This can be seen in other passages in the Bible (Rom. 14:9, Phil. 2:5–9).

Whatever we know about Jesus, his sufferings, and his glory, that is how much we will understand the Bible, no more.

These are the two main aspects of the mediation of Jesus and his kingdom, and the order they come to the church: first sufferings and then glory: "If we endure [suffer], we will also reign with him" (2 Tim. 2:12). Those who try any other way deceive themselves. Some would rather reign here in this world, to which we can say, "And would that you did reign, so that we might share the rule with you!" (1 Cor. 4:8). But the members of the spiritual body must be conformed to the Head. In him, sufferings came before glory, and so they must be with us. The order in Satan's kingdom is the opposite: first the good things of this life, and then eternal misery (Luke 16:25).

These are the two fountains of the salvation of the church—the two anointed ones that stand before the Lord and from whom the golden oil flows to dedicate and sanctify the church to God. This glory of Jesus in his exaltation, which followed after his sufferings, is what we look at now.

From Man to Exalted One

This is the glory that Jesus prays his disciples may be able to see. It is where all the other parts of his glory are revealed; the evidence, promise, and way they are all shown. All the examples of his glory already spoken of were hidden, a veil drawn over them while he was in this world. So, many did not see any of it, and even if they did, it was obscured. But in this glory, that veil is taken off so that the whole glory of his person and his mediation is wonderfully displayed. When we see this glory, we will see him as he is. This is the glory the Father gave him before the foundation of the world, and which he received when he ascended.

By this glory, we do not understand the glory of his godly nature or as "God over all, blessed forever" (Rom. 9:5), but the manifestation of this glory, after it had been veiled in this world under the "form of a servant," (Phil. 2:7) is found here. The divine glory of Jesus in his person does not belong to his exaltation but is revealed in it. He did not leave it while he was in this world, but the direct evidence and declaration of it he put aside until he was "declared to be the Son of God in power" by the resurrection from the dead (Rom. 1:4).

When the sun was completely eclipsed, his beauty, light, and glory still shone. He is still the same as he was from the beginning—a "great light to rule the day." To us, he appears as a dark, useless meteor, but when he leaves his orbit to freely come to us, he manifests his natural light and glory. This is how it was with the divine nature of Jesus. He veiled the glory of it by taking on the flesh, our nature to be his own, to become the "form of a servant," someone without status. Now that this temporary eclipse is finished, it shines down in its infinite brilliance and beauty, showing the present exaltation of who he is. When those who saw him as a poor, sorrowful, persecuted man, dying on the cross, came to see him in all the infinite glories of the divine nature revealed in him, it filled their hearts with supernatural joy and admiration. This is why he prayed for the disciples when he was on the earth, that they might see his glory because he knew it would satisfy them eternally.

We cannot fully grasp the glorification of the human nature of Jesus—his soul and body that lived and died, suffered, and rose again—but it is important to look at it since he will bring all those who believe in him to it.

His Nature Is Exalted

That nature he took on in this world, is exalted into glory. Some people deny that he has either flesh or blood in heaven, but the foundation of Christianity is that he was made flesh, that he did become flesh and blood. It is wrong to believe he rejected the flesh and blood that he became in the womb of Mary—a body he lived and died in, offered as a sacrifice to God, and rose from the dead in. This is not the true nature of the glorification of the humanity of Jesus. We cannot understand it completely, his complete nature, but that he is still in the same human nature he had on the earth—soul, and body—is a fundamental belief of the Christian faith.

His Nature Is Divine

This nature of Jesus the man is filled with all the divine attributes that a limited, created nature can have. It is not deified, it is not made a god—it does not combine in heaven into one nature, and is not omniscient, omnipresent, omnipotent—but it is exalted in all godly perfection above the glory of angels and men. It is incomprehensibly closer to God than all of them—it communicates with God in glorious light, love, and power above them all, but it is still a creature.

This glory of Jesus' human nature is what all believers will share because when we see him as he is, we will be like him. However, his glory is still above all that we share. "There is one glory of the sun, and another glory of the moon, and another glory of the stars; for star differs from star in glory" (1 Cor. 15:41). If there is a difference in glory among the stars, how much more is there between the glory of the sun and any other star! This is the difference that is and will be to eternity, between the human nature of Jesus and what glorified believers will achieve.

The Exaltation of Christ

But this is not the glory in his exaltation that comes after his humiliation and death. It consists of these things:

1. **Exalted over creation.** The exaltation of human nature, existing in the divine person, above all creation in power, dignity, authority, and rule, with everything God has given to show the beauty of its glory. This is explained in Hebrews 1:2-3.
2. **Exalted by the Father.** The evidence of the Father's love for him, and his delight in him, as he fulfills his role. So, he is said to sit "at the right hand of God" (Rom. 8:4). The glory and dignity of Jesus in his exaltation is incredible; the highest given to a creature is contained in this verse.
3. **Glorious as Mediator.** The full revelation of his own divine wisdom, love, and grace in his redemption of the church. This glory is only for him as angels and men have no interest in it. Here, it is not clearly seen, but above, it shines

in its brightness, to the eternal joy of those who see him.

This is the glory Jesus prayed that his disciples might see and know. This is what we should strive after in faith—faith, not imagination. Arrogant, foolish people who have conventional ideas of this glory know nothing of its real nature. They have tried to represent it in pictures and images, with all the beauty that art, gold, and jewels of ornaments can give them. This is the representation of the present glory of Jesus that appeals to the imagination and emotions of superstitious people, like many religious churches. They do not know the Bible or the eternal glory of the Son of God.

The glory that Jesus has in heaven cannot be seen or understood in this world, only in the light of faith fixing itself on divine revelation. The steady exercise of faith in the revelation and description of this glory in the Bible is the foundation, rule, and measure, of all holy meditations.

Our Duty and Privilege

Ask yourself these questions to hold yourself accountable in your efforts to see this glory:

- When did you see it clearly?
- When you saw it, was your heart satisfied and refreshed?

It is one of the main pillars of our faith, bringing us joy, an object of our hope, a place of comfort—our greatest encouragement in obedience and suffering.

- Is your mind thinking of these things every day?
- Are you not really concerned about it?
- Do you look at it as something we will one day understand fully when we are in heaven?

Many people do not care where Jesus is or what he is, hoping to be saved by him without knowing. They hope and pretend that they will see him and his glory in heaven, but they actually do not expect anything. Those who do not want to see the glory of Jesus in this world will never see him fully in glory in heaven. They have no desire, just looking for relief from this world. It is only by faith, which they despise or totally neglect.

Constantly meditating on this glory of Jesus will fill us with joy because it is an effective motivation. We are naturally selfish, only looking after our own concerns, yet he forgives and saves us even though we do not think of him. This attitude is opposite to faith and love, which always puts Jesus above us, and our concerns in him above all our own. This should stir us to think about this glory.

- Who is exalted overall?
- Who is clothed in glory, majesty, and power?
- Who sits at the right hand of the Majesty on high, all his enemies as his footstool?
- Is it not he who was poor, despised, persecuted, and killed for our sake?

- Is it not Jesus who loved us, gave himself for us, and washed us in his own blood?

So, Peter told the Jews that the same "Jesus, whom you killed by hanging him on a tree. God exalted him at his right hand as Leader and Savior, to give repentance to Israel and forgiveness of sins" (Acts 5:30-31). If we value his love, if we have any concern for what he has done and suffered for the church, then we will rejoice in his present state and glory.

Let the world rage as it wants. Let it set itself in its power against everything of Jesus. Let people make themselves drunk with the blood of Christians. We have this to oppose them and support ourselves: Jesus says, "Fear not, I am the first and the last, and the living one. I died, and behold I am alive forevermore, and I have the keys of Death and Hades" (Rev. 1:17-18).

Wonderful Jesus, we can add nothing to you, nothing to your glory. It is a joy for us that you are what you are—that you are so gloriously exalted at the right hand of God. We long to see that glory more clearly, according to your prayer and promise.

Study Guide - Reflections

Some religious churches have crucifixes on their walls. This is not a bad thing since we should always be reminded of the cross of Christ and what he did for us—the ultimate sacrifice and act of love. But we can set up camp there and never go any further than the hill of Calvary. Jesus never came simply to die. He came to defeat death and rise again so we may have life in him. Without the resurrection, the cross makes him another martyr.

It was because he accomplished the work in full that God exalted him, lifted him up to his place of glory and honor. Christ suffered so that he may be glorified, and he was an example to us to do the same. We cannot have life without first dying, and it is pointless to die if there is no life after it. Those Christians who have spiritual life know this; they are not afraid to die physically but also to die to themselves, because the resurrection life of Jesus fills them daily.

1. Read Philippians 3:10. How does Paul say we should know Jesus?
2. Do you thank and praise God for dying on the cross? Do you also thank and praise him for rising again? Do you go further to thank and praise him for ascending to his rightful place in heaven?
3. In what ways is Jesus exalted?
4. Why is Satan and the world so against this exaltation of Jesus?
5. Owen makes an interesting comment at the end: "We can add nothing to you, nothing to your glory." What does this mean?

8

THE GLORY OF CHRIST IN THE OLD TESTAMENT

Beginning at Moses and all the prophets, he declared unto his disciples in all the Scriptures the things concerning himself.
–Luke 24:27

All of these testify to Jesus and his glory. This is the line of life and light running through the whole Old Testament. Without it, we can understand nothing properly, and ignoring it makes us as blind as the Jews when reading the books—a veil is over their minds. It is only faith—discovering the glory of Jesus—that can remove that veil of darkness that covers people's minds when reading the Old Testament (2 Cor. 3:14–16). Let us look at some of the ways in which the glory of Jesus was represented to believers in the Old Testament.

In Rituals of the Law

We see it in the beautiful Old Testament rituals of worship that are far better than all the amazing ceremonies invented by people—they were designed to represent the glory of Jesus, in his person and his role. No human invention can do this—we cannot create mysteries or give anything natural a spiritual significance, but this is how it was in the old institutions. What were the tabernacle and the temple? What was the oracle, the ark, the cherubim, and the mercy seat in the holy place? What was the high priest with all his robes and rituals? What were the sacrifices and annual sprinkling of blood in the most holy place? What was the whole system of this religious worship? They were all representations of Jesus in the glory of his person and role. They were a shadow, and the body represented by that shadow was Jesus, as seen in Hebrews 9. The main purpose of it was, "Moses was faithful in all God's house as a servant, to testify to the things that were to be spoken later" (Heb. 3:5). Everything Moses did in building the Tabernacle and instituting the rituals was all to represent the things of Jesus that were later revealed. It was the same in the ministry of the prophets (1 Pet. 1:11-12).

In the Song of Songs

We see it in his relationship with the church. It is shown in many parts of the Bible, but Song of Songs is a dedicated record of Jesus' words of love and grace to his church, with their replies of love to him and delight in him. We can see the benefit of having a close, loving relationship with Jesus when the words we speak to him bring light and life to our minds in all their power. But because many do not understand it so well, this book is often ignored, even despised because they see its expressions as too offensive.

The representation of the glory of Jesus in rituals of worship, combined with this intimate relationship they had with Jesus in grace, faith, and love, gives us a hint of the view they had of his glory. What holy joy and admiration, sacred satisfaction, passionate love, and diligence are found in a relationship with him—this discovery of the glory of Jesus found in the hearts of believers is graphically expressed in this book. Having this attitude for a few days or hours is a blessing that surpasses all the treasures of the earth. If we have revelations of the same glory that exceed those of the believers in the Old Testament, but we do not have the same passion when it comes to Jesus, or a continuous admiration of his attributes, we will one day be judged as unworthy to have received them.

In His Appearances

We also see it in the Old Testament, when he appeared to certain important biblical people. This was a prelude to his incarnation. He was still God then but appeared in the shape of a man to signify what he would be. He did not create a human nature and combine it with his. It was purely through his divine power that he took the form of a man only to leave it soon after. This is how he appeared to Abraham, Jacob, Moses, Joshua, and others. Because he was the divine person living in and with the Old Testament church, he also assumed human emotions to show that one day he would do so as a man. After the fall, God's dealings with the church in the Old Testament are linked to the future incarnation of Christ. It would be silly to think God could grieve, repent, get angry, and be pleased unless he intended to take on the nature that exhibits those emotions.

In the Prophets

We see it in prophetic visions. John talks about the vision Isaiah had of Jesus when he saw his glory (John 12:41). And it was a wonderful sight: his divine person exalted on a throne of glory as "his train filled the temple" (Isa. 6:1). The whole train of his glorious grace filled the temple of his body. This is the true tabernacle, which God built, not man—the temple that was destroyed, and which he raised again in three days, where the fullness of the Godhead lives (Col. 2: 9). This was the glory that filled him with fear and awe, and that the glorious one brought him relief when he took away his iniquity with a coal from the altar (Isa. 6:1–5). This was the purifying power of his sacrifice. This was food for the believers' hearts so they could lift their voices and cry, "Make haste, my beloved, and be like a gazelle or a young stag on the mountains of spices" (Song. 8:14).

The same glorious appearance was seen on Mount Sinai when the law was given (Exod. 19, Ps. 68:17-18), and hinted at by Paul concerning the ascension of Jesus after his resurrection (Eph. 4:8). When he brought the law, it was in fiery terror, but the Psalmist describes him in that moment as full of mercy. Because of its holiness, the law was like a death to the people along with the harshness of the curse, but when he fulfilled it, he brought life through forgiveness and righteousness.

His incarnation was revealed, although not so clearly as in the Gospel. We see an example of this in Isaiah's prophecy:

For to us a child is born, to us a son is given; and the government shall be upon his shoulder, and his name shall be called Wonderful Counselor, Mighty God, Everlasting Father, Prince of Peace. Of the increase of his government and of peace there will be no end, on the throne of David and over his kingdom, to establish it and to uphold it with justice and with righteousness from this time forth and forevermore. The zeal of the Lord of hosts will do this. (Isa. 9:6-7)

This is enough to confuse all the Jews and other enemies of the glory of Jesus. Even though they searched for this truth, they could not see or understand how it would happen. But now, it is clear to us in the Gospel, and so, it is blindness for those who refuse to believe it. Their pride which has no spiritual wisdom, blinds them from the light of this truth.

Promises, prophecies, predictions, about his person, his coming, his role, his kingdom, and his glory, with the wisdom, grace, and love of God to the church in him, are the lifeline that runs through the whole of the Old Testament. Jesus used Moses and the prophets to teach his disciples all these things, saying "Search the Scriptures because... it is they that bear witness about me" (John 5:39). If we do not find them, if we do not discern them there, it is because a veil of blindness is over our minds. We cannot get any advantage when we read, study, or meditate on the Old Testament unless we see the glory of Jesus in it.

In Metaphors

The glory of Jesus is also seen in metaphorical expressions in the Old Testament. These help our minds to see things that are hard to understand. God, in his wisdom, shows us the power of spiritual things in ways we can naturally discern. Examples of this are when Jesus was likened to animals and nature to represent the power and brilliance in him. He is also called a rose, because of the sweet aroma of his love, grace, and obedience—a lily, because of his gracious beauty and gentleness—the pearl of great price, because of his worth to those who believe he is precious—the vine, for his fruitfulness—the lion, for his power—the lamb, for his meekness and willingness to be a sacrifice.

Study Guide - Reflections

As born-again Christians under the New Covenant of grace, we tend to lean heavily on the New Testament for our guidance and teaching. The Old is largely left aside unless we want to dip our toes into the waters of Psalms, find some quick quotes from Proverbs, or pick up on one of the all-time favorite Bible stories like Noah and Jonah. Otherwise, we give a wide detour when it comes to the dry, dusty legalism of Leviticus or the heavy judgment of Jeremiah. If we're honest, we want to be uplifted, not dragged down, and so, we favor the scriptures that we're comfortable with.

But here, we see that the Bible isn't really split into two separate parts. Yes, there are two covenants, and there are two dispensations, but they are all part of God's plan. And if we open our eyes, we will see Jesus, redemption, salvation, and God's love woven like a thread right from Genesis to Revelation. All the prophets, the priests, and the kings looked to the promise of and glory of Jesus, and we should do the same.

1. How often do you read the Old Testament or do you stick to the New most times?
2. Does your church or pastor ever refer to the Old Testament when preaching as a means to reveal Jesus and the cross?
3. Why did God find it necessary to reveal Jesus and his glory to the people of the Old Testament in a veiled, obscure way?
4. What is the difference between the way they saw it and how we see it today?
5. If you want to learn and see more of Jesus in the Old Testament, a good book to read is *Christ in the Old Testament* by Charles Spurgeon.

9

THE GLORY OF CHRIST IN THE CHURCH

Here, we look at three things pertaining to Jesus' glory in his relation to the church.

The intimate relationship between Jesus and the church is just and equal in the sight of God, according to the rules of his eternal righteousness—what he did and suffered is credited to us, with all its blessings, as if we had done and suffered the same things ourselves. This relationship of his with us was an act of his own mind and will, and in it he is glorious.

The enemies of the glory of Jesus and of his cross take this for granted—that there should be such a relationship between the guilty and he that suffers for that person, that in Jesus the guilty somehow experience the punishment. They claim that there was no such relationship between Jesus and sinners—none at all; he was only a man like us or that he was not like us at all. These false claims ignore the Bible in its fullness through subtle deceit.

Peter tells us that "He himself bore our sins in his body on the tree" and that he "suffered once for sins, the righteous for the unrighteous, that he might bring us to God" (1 Peter 2:24, 3:18). But this might seem strange to our logic. How can it be justice that the just should suffer for the unjust? Where is divine righteousness in this? For it was an act of God: "The LORD has laid on him the iniquity of us all" (Isa. 53:6). The justice in this can be looked at further.

First, all the chosen, the church, fell through Adam under the curse because of the transgression of the law. In this curse was physical and eternal death. No one could have this curse and be saved. And because of the righteousness, holiness, and truth of God, this sin could not go unpunished. For God to save his church, there had to be a transfer of punishment from those who deserved it and could not bear it to one who had not deserved it but could bear it.

This translation of punishment through divine intervention is the foundation of Christianity, of everything in the Bible. This was shown in the first promise and later explained and confirmed through the rituals of the Old Testament. In the sacrifices of the law, there was a revival of the greatest and most fundamental principle of nature—that God is to be worshiped—however, the main reason was to show this translation of punishment from one offender to another, who would be a sacrifice in his place.

Let us look at the justice and glory of Jesus in the following points:

Taking On Punishment and Justice

It is not contrary to holy justice or the principles of man's goodness, that a person should suffer punishment for the sins and offenses of others.

God confirms that he will bring "the iniquity of the fathers on the children to the third and the fourth generation" (Exod. 20:5). Children are also sinners, continuing in their fathers' sins. The worst sinner must be dealt with accordingly. But it would be unjust to punish them for their fathers' sins while claiming it is unlawful to punish someone for another person's sin.

"Our fathers sinned, and are no more; and we bear their iniquities" (Lam. 5:7). Through the Babylon exile, God punished the people for the sins of their forefathers, especially those committed in the days of Manasseh (2 Kings 23:26-27). And in the final destruction of that nation, God punished them for the guilt of all bloody persecutions from the beginning of the world (Luke 11:50-51).

Canaan was cursed for the sin of his father (Gen. 9:25). Saul's seven sons were put to death for their father's bloody cruelty (2 Sam. 21:9, 14). For the sin of David, seventy thousand were destroyed by an angel, as David said, "Behold, I have sinned, and I have done wickedly. But these sheep, what have they done?" (2 Sam. 24:15-17, see also 1 Kings 21:29). It was the same with everyone who perished in the flood, or at Sodom and Gomorrah. There are many other examples.

So, there is no inconsistency with this holy justice or

human rules, that the sins of some may be punished on others.

The Requirement

We can see that this administration of justice is also not random—that anyone can be punished for the sins of others. There is always a cause and reason for it, a link between those who sin and those who are punished for their sins. There are two things here:

1. There is a special relationship for this translation of punishment just as that between parents and children, or between a king and subjects, as in the case of David. Here we see the people sinning and those suffering referred to as one body, where one member might sin and another will suffer because of it.
2. It consists of mutual interest. Those whose sins are punished through others have an invested interest as if the punishment is done to them. Therefore, these sinners are threatened with the punishment and evil that come on their children because of what they have done: "Your children shall be shepherds in the wilderness forty years and shall suffer for your faithlessness" (Num. 14:33). The punishment due to their sins is partly transferred to their children, and the sting of their own punishment was felt in this.

Joined With the Church

There is a greater, more intimate relation, a higher mutual interest, between Jesus and the church, than any other; where it was just and equal in God's sight that he should suffer for us, and that what he did and suffered would be credited to us.

In this, we see three things: natural, moral (spiritual), and mutual joining. In each of these, Jesus relates to his church.

Naturally Joined

Naturally, God has made all mankind one (Acts 17:26) —where we are all linked together. So, we are all (brothers, sisters, or neighbors) to show love and kindness to one another (Luke 10:36). This same relationship was between Jesus and the church, as the Bible shows:

Since therefore the children share in flesh and blood, he himself likewise partook of the same things, that through death he might destroy the one who has the power of death, that is, the devil, and deliver all those who through fear of death were subject to lifelong slavery," so "he who sanctifies and those who are sanctified all have one source. (Heb. 2:11-15)

In stepping down to earth and taking on our human form, he shared our nature. We see two things in this:

1. This relationship between Jesus and the church did not come from the necessity of nature but from a voluntary act of his will. The

relationship we all share with each other is necessary. Every person is another's brother or sister because we are human. Natural inheritance makes us all part of the same nature without a choice. It was different for Jesus because he became flesh and blood and entered this association with us through his own free will. It was his own choice. This relationship of Jesus in human form with the church is different from the one we all share with one another. While a human suffering in someone's place could not satisfy holy judgment, because we are all related, it was different for Jesus, who came into this relationship through his own will.

2. He came in for one reason: that through taking on our nature, he might suffer what was to be suffered for the church. That is why it says, "that through death he might destroy the one who has the power of death, that is, the devil, and deliver all those who through fear of death were subject to lifelong slavery" (Heb. 2:14-15). This was the only reason for his relationship in nature with the church.

It is pointless to argue that being of the same nature as humans is not enough to allow the righteousness of punishing one for another, and that Jesus, being of the same nature as his church is not enough for him to suffer for us in our place. Through an act of his own will and choice, he took on our nature so that he might suffer for us. There is nothing to compare with this relationship between Christ and the church, and that is why he is glorious and precious to those who believe.

Spiritually Joined

There is a supernatural link between Jesus and the church which fulfills the strictest moral relationships between people or things. We see it between the head of a body and its members, or the tree of the vine and its branches, or a husband and wife. This relationship between Jesus and his church is clearly seen in the Bible and is the reason for his suffering in its place. Paul says, "Husbands, love your wives, as Christ loved the church,"—his wife and bride—"and gave himself up for her" (Eph. 5:25–32). Being the head and husband of the church, which was to be sanctified and saved only by his blood and suffering, it was righteous also that what he suffered should be credited to those for whom he suffered. The enemies of Jesus' glory try to compare the relationship between him and the church with their own human examples, trying to explain why he suffered for us. But his glory remains a mystery to them because it can only be spiritually understood.

This spiritual union of Jesus with his church is significant to what he suffered because it results in people turning to him and being born again. It is by faith that we are established in him. Until that is worked in us, we have no spiritual union with him. He is not a head or a husband for unsanctified unbelievers who remain in their unbelief, and this was the state of the church when Jesus suffered for us (Rom. 5:8, Eph. 2:5). The church is the effect of the work of redemption, not the object.

1. Although this spiritual union is not actually complete without the Holy Spirit, the church was designed before he suffered to be his bride so that he might love her and suffer for her. "Israel served for a wife, and for a wife he guarded sheep" (Hos. 12:12). He was not his wife until after he had worked for her, and paid the price to be his wife, yet he called her his wife while he worked for her, because of his love for her, and because she was created to be his wife once he finished his work. The church was created to be the spouse of Jesus where he loved her and gave himself for her. The redemption of the church was the reason the church became the bride of Christ because of the power of the union as Paul describes (Eph. 5:25–27).
2. Before Jesus suffered for the church, there was a supreme act of the will of God the Father, giving all the chosen to him, entrusting them to him, to be redeemed, sanctified, and saved (John 17:6-9, 10:14–16). This spiritual union between Jesus and the church has its power in this before it actually comes to be.

Mutually Joined

There is a mutual union between people, depending on the contract they have entered. They agree that one person will stand as a guarantee to do and answer what is required to achieve the purpose of the covenant. So, Jesus became the guarantee of the new covenant on behalf of the church (Heb. 7:22), submitting himself to

God to suffer for them in their place, so that they might be sanctified and saved. This spiritual union was just and equal in the sight of God so that what Jesus suffered should be imputed to us and is now completed.

The mystery of taking on the sins of the church—the guilt and punishment of sinners onto one who is completely innocent, pure, and righteous—is the life, soul, and center of all biblical revelations. In this, Jesus is incredibly glorious and precious to all who believe. No heart can conceive, no tongue can express the glory of Christ in this.

The Glory of this Doctrine

Let us look at some of the effects of his condescension and love:

First, it shines in the righteousness of God through the forgiveness of sins. The divine nature is seen in justice, punishing sins according to what they deserve. From the beginning we see God dispensing eternal punishment of the angels that sinned and throwing Adam out of Paradise. Now, the church, God's chosen, are also sinners—through Adam.

What happens to God's justice for them? Can it leave them unpunished? What about the justice that did not spare the angels or Adam? The righteousness of God and the forgiveness of sin seem so contradictory, causing many to stumble and fall. (See Rom. 10:3-4).

But Jesus' intervention, taking on the punishment of the church because of his relationship with them, is where the righteousness of God and the forgiveness of sins find harmony—a wonderful picture of his eternal glory.

By virtue of his union with the church, through his own will before God, it was righteous for God to lay the punishment of all our sins upon him so that he could forgive them, and honor his justice, grace, and mercy (Rom. 3:24–26).

Here we see a divine act of justice and mercy: one in punishing, the other forgiving. This apparent inconsistency between the righteousness of God and the salvation of sinners, which confuses many, is removed and taken away in this one act of Jesus. On the cross, godly holiness and justice were fulfilled; and through his resurrection, grace and mercy are realized. This is the glory that fills the hearts and satisfies the souls of those who believe. What more can they desire, what else can bring peace and comfort to their souls, than seeing God eternally pleased in the declaration of his righteousness and the exercise of his mercy, to bring their salvation?

Secondly, Jesus is glorious in his obedience and fulfillment of the law of God. What could be further from divine perfection than to give a law which could not be fulfilled by those to whom it was given, or those who could benefit from it? This could not be done by us. But through the obedience of Jesus, in his union with the church, the law was fulfilled in us by being fulfilled for us and obtaining the eternal rewards of it for us. (See Rom. 8:3-4).

Through faith, one view of this glory of Jesus will scatter all fear, answer all objections, and give relief to despondent, poor, tempted, doubting souls. It will be an anchor for all believers to hold them firm and steadfast in all trials, storms, and temptations in life and death.

Study Guide - Reflections

We are the church. It is not a building, a holy site, or any man-made structure, but a spiritual body with Jesus as the head. Everyone who believes is a part of that body, that family. We have been chosen and set apart by God as his redeemed people. And, it has nothing to do with us... we do not deserve this honor in any way or form. It is God, it is his grace that has reached out across the void and called us to be his own. If any glory is in the church, then it is all his!

Christians may not be perfect, and finding a church that has everything going right for it is impossible. We are humans, all relying on God's guidance and sanctification. We will only be perfect on that side of heaven. But for now, we are a reflection of his love, salvation, and grace; we are a testimony of his wonderful work of renewal, of people being transformed into his image. One look at a spirit-filled bunch of Christians following Jesus, and you will see something of his glory in that relationship.

1. Why did Jesus have to suffer in your place and take your punishment? What does this mean for you now?
2. What does it mean to be chosen, elected, and set apart? Do you feel chosen by God?

3. Why is the church called a bride, and why is this an excellent metaphor? Read 2 Corinthians 11:2 and Revelation 21:2.
4. What three ways is Jesus joined to us?
5. Do you see any of Jesus' glory in your own church?

10

THE GLORY OF CHRIST TO BELIEVERS

Another aspect of Jesus' glory that we need to see by faith is the mysterious impartation of himself and all the benefits of his mediation to our hearts for our present happiness and future eternal favor.

In this way, Jesus becomes ours as we are his. This is the life, glory, and consolation of the church (Song. 6:3, 2:16, 7:10) because of our spiritual union. There is a reason for this relation between him and the church, where he is theirs, and they are his. He is in them, and they are in him, in a way not between him and other people in the world.

Paul, speaking of this union says that it is a "mystery" for "I am saying that it refers to Christ and the church" (Eph. 5:32).

Jesus does not show himself to all the same way the sun shines equally on the whole world, nor is he with everyone because of his omnipresence, nor through some transmission of his soul into everyone, nor does he become ours by eating bread and drinking wine in communion. This mystery comes from, and depends on, other reasons which we will look at.

But before we do, there is another way Jesus is with the church, which we see in divine communications and their glory. To do this, we must look at the harmony and correspondence between the old creation (the earth) and the new (Christians).

Through Creation

1. All power, goodness, and wisdom are found in God. And in them, with everything else of his nature, is his glory.
2. The old creation was God's goodness through almighty power, directed by infinite wisdom to reveal that glory (Ps. 19:1, Rom. 1:20). Everything depended on one another, without which they could not subsist or continue. There is an order, and all creatures on the earth live off the earth to survive, depending on the sun and other heavenly bodies, as God declares, "I will answer, declares the Lord, I will answer the heavens, and they shall answer the earth, and the earth shall answer the grain, the wine, and the oil, and they shall answer Jezreel" (Hos. 2:21-22).
3. In this mutual dependency, they all depend on and are influenced by God himself: the eternal fountain of being, power, and goodness. Maintaining this order through constant divine

communication of being, goodness, and power, God is glorified just as much as the day he created everything (Acts 14:15-17, 17:24-29).
4. This glory of God is visible and obvious to us because, from his creation and provision, we learn his eternal power and Godhead, where he is essentially glorious.
5. God did not only intend to glorify himself through his nature, but also in the three persons of Father, Son, and Spirit. Even though all creation came through the power and goodness in the person of the Father, as he is the fountain of the Trinity (the Creator), yet the work of creation was from the Son, and the power and wisdom of the Father (John 1:1-3, Col. 1:16, Heb. 1:2). The whole of creation was under the Spirit's care, to preserve and help produce different creatures (Gen. 1:2)—and as it continues, the same Spirit operates in all things. Nothing can survive on its own, without continual power from him. (Ps. 104:29-30).

By these divine impartations, in making and preserving all living things, God shows his glory through nature. But it is even better, though not physically visible, in the new creation, as we will see.

Through Christians

1. All goodness, grace, life, light, mercy, and power, the causes of the new creation, are all originally in God, in his divine nature. He is

eternally glorious in them, and the whole design of the new creation was to reveal his glory in them, through impartation.
2. The first impartation is to Jesus, the Head of the church. It pleased God that in him all the fullness of these things should dwell so that the new creation might consist in him (Col. 1:17–19).
3. This impartation was made to him as a source of all that goodness, grace, life, light, power, and mercy necessary for the new creation to continue and live. They were put in him, to be hidden in him, to live in him. From him, they were to be transmitted to the spiritual body—the church. This is the first channel of divine power and wisdom, for his glory to be revealed in the new creation. Jesus is the head, treasuring up in him all that was necessary for its growth and life, as the church is chosen in him for grace and glory. He is the well of divine glory in every other transmission that follows.
4. This impartation to Jesus is (1) to his person; and then, (2) as Christ. It is in the person of Christ that all fullness originally dwells. On taking on human nature as the Son of God, all fullness dwells in him physically (Col. 2:9). And when he received the Spirit in all fullness, all wisdom and knowledge were also in him (Col. 2:3), and he was filled with the unsearchable riches of divine grace (Eph. 3:8–11). The role of Christ is the way God intended to transmit the treasures of grace that were conveyed to his person. This is Jesus' role as a

priest, prophet, and king—nothing else but a way to impart the grace in his person to the church. We have only managed to scratch the surface of the full spiritual glory in this.

5. Election prepared the new creation. In the old creation, God first prepared and created everything which was then formed into different beings by the power of the Holy Spirit. In the new creation, God prepared and set apart a portion of mankind according to his will. Out of this, the Holy Spirit would shape and mold the glorious church. What the Psalmist said of the physical body is also true of the spiritual body of Christ.

My frame was not hidden from you, when I was being made in secret, intricately woven in the depths of the earth. Your eyes saw my unformed substance; in your book were written, every one of them, the days that were formed for me, when as yet there was none of them. (Ps. 139:15-16)

The substance of the church was under the eye of God, as proposed in the decree of election, but it was still imperfect. It was not formed or shaped into members of the spiritual body, but they were all written in the Book of Life. According to God's purposes, the Holy Spirit has molded them into the shape designed for them.

6. This is the order of spiritual impartation. From the infinite, eternal spring of wisdom, grace, goodness, and love, in the Father—all

treasured up in the person and mediation of the Son—the Holy Spirit communicates life, light, power, grace, and mercy to all who are part of the new creation. This is where God glorifies his nature—his infinite wisdom, power, goodness, and grace—as the only eternal spring of all these things, and his existence in three persons. This is the glorious truth of the Trinity—which some oppose, neglect, or see as above them or not belonging to them—that is precious to those who believe, the foundation of their faith and hope. Seeing the glorious order of those divine impartations, we understand the glory of the nature of God in the three persons of Father, Son, and Holy Spirit.

7. According to this order, the Holy Spirit moves and acts on the new creation, formed and animated with spiritual life, light, grace, and power, for the glory of God. They are not called accidentally, according to things they have done or said, but in every age, at his own time and season, the Holy Spirit gives these things to those chosen for the glory of God.

8. In the same way, the new creation is preserved every day—every moment of living power, mercy, and grace, is relayed in this order to all believers in the world. A continual influence comes from the Fountain, from the Head, into all the members, so they all consist in him, are worked by him, who does so for his own good pleasure. Paul says that the whole constitution of church order is a physical instrument, to

promote this divine transmission to all the members of the church (Eph. 4:13–15).

This is the order of divine impartation, which continues in heaven for all eternity, because God is, and ever will be, all, and in all. But now, it is invisible to our physical eyes and our human logic. That is why many despise it because they see no glory in it. But let us look at Paul's prayer so we may not be like that (Eph. 1:16–23). The revelation of the glory of God in the old creation is nowhere near as wonderful and glorious as the new.

Moving from this general overview of divine impartation, we will look specifically at the way Jesus imparts himself, with all the blessings of his mediation, to us who believe.

The Father's Eternal Plan

We receive him by faith (John 1:12). When we receive him, he must be given to us through divine acts of the Father, and of his own.

It is all rooted in the will, pleasure, and grace of the Father. This is the order and method for all divine acts of grace. They all come from him and, having achieved their goals, they return to him again (Eph. 1:4–6). When Jesus is made ours, transmitted to us, it is a free act of the Father (1 Cor. 1:30, Rom. 5:15–17). In this, we also see the following working together:

1. His eternal purpose is to glorify his grace in his chosen people, through Jesus and the benefits of his mediation (Eph. 1:2).

2. He gave all the chosen to Jesus, to be his own, to suffer for them: "Yours they were, and you gave them to me" (John 17:6).
3. The promise, or Gospel, where Jesus' contribution, an interest in him and all that he is, is given to believers (John 1:12, 1 John 1:1-4).
4. An act of almighty power, working and creating faith in the hearts of Christians, enabling them to receive Jesus revealed and communicated to them by the Gospel (Eph. 1:19-20, 2:5-8).

These have an influence on the glory of Jesus because this impartation of him to the church is because of the counsel, wisdom, grace, and power of the Father.

The Gift of the Son

But the acts of Jesus himself are what we want to look at, those which manifest the glory of his wisdom, love, and condescension.

His Holy Spirit

He gives his Holy Spirit to us—the Holy Spirit as given to him by the Father, living in him. This Spirit he gives to all believers, to also live in them (John 14:14–20, 1 Cor. 6:17, Rom. 8:9). So, there is a union between him and them. In his incarnation, he took our nature into personal union with his own, and here he takes us into a spiritual union with himself. He becomes ours, and we are his.

In this, he is glorious. The same Spirit in him as the head, and the church as his body, animating the whole, is a supernatural effect of godly wisdom. There is nothing of this nature in creation—no union or mutual communication like it. The purest unions in nature cannot compare (Eph. 5:25-32). In this way, Jesus is precious to us, but a stumbling block and a rock of offense to the disobedient. This glorious result of his wisdom and grace, this strange way of transmitting himself to the church, is despised by many. They understand being joined to a woman means becoming one flesh, but they do not understand being joined to the Lord to become one spirit. But this principle of the spiritual life of the church, and all growth in God, where your "life is hidden with Christ in God," is the glory, the exaltation, the honor, and safety of the church, for the praise of the grace of God (Col. 3:3). To understand its causes, effects, methods, and blessings, is better all the wisdom in the world.

A New Nature in Him

He transmits himself to us through a new nature, his own nature, in us. So, the same spiritual nature is in him and in the church. The only difference is that in him it is completely perfect, while in the church it is in different stages, according to how he gives it to us. But the same divine nature is in him and us because the promises of the Gospel make us participants of his Divine nature. It is not enough for us that he has taken our nature to be his unless he also gives us his nature to be ours. He puts all those gracious characteristics in our hearts which he had in his human nature. This is the new man, new creature, divine nature, spirit born of the Spirit, transformation into his image, putting him on, and worship of God we are created for, that the Bible speaks about (John 3:6, Rom 6:3–8, 2 Cor. 3:18, 5:17, Eph. 4:20–24, 2 Peter 1:4).

This new heavenly nature formed in us is the first act of the union between Jesus and us by the Spirit living in us, his nature. We are predestined to conform to his image, so it is worked and produced in our hearts by his power, character, and efficiency.

This is a most heavenly way of giving himself to us, where he becomes our wisdom and sanctification. (1 Cor. 1:30). He says, "This at last is bone of my bones and flesh of my flesh" (Gen. 2:23)—I see myself, my own nature, in them, and this makes them acceptable. In this way, "he might present the church to himself in splendor, without spot or wrinkle or any such thing, that she might be holy and without blemish" (Eph. 5:27). This impartation of Jesus to us, forming his own nature in us, contains all the purity, beauty, holiness, and inner glory of the church. This is what separates it from the world and distinguishes it from those who only practice outward religious rituals. These are the first fruits, showing his image in the world, and this is how Jesus is glorified.

He Joins Us to Himself

He also does this by establishing us in himself, which he does through his own work by faith. We see two things as a result: the grace or power of the Gospel and the law or constitution of the Gospel. Both have a great influence on this spiritual impartation of Jesus to the church.

The first of these provides us with spiritual life, sustenance, motion, strength in grace, and perseverance from him continually. This he teaches us in the parable of the vine and its branches (John 15:1-5). In this, there is a continual transmission of grace to the church and everyone in it for all spiritual life. Although we are alive, it is not us, but Christ who lives in us, and the life which we lead in the flesh is by the faith of the Son of God. And the other—from the law of the Gospel—his righteousness and all the blessings of his mediation are given to us as Paul describes (Rom. 3-5).

This mutual relationship between Jesus and us by love is how he transmits his love to us in our hearts by the Holy Spirit. Our love for him is worked in us by the power of the same Spirit, and there is a deep wonderful glory in that too. There are also the benefits of his role as Christ that flow to us, all the benefits of his mediation that we share in. But this look at the glory of Jesus in his spiritual impartation of himself to his church is enough to give us a view of it that will fill our hearts with holy admiration and thanksgiving.

Study Guide - Reflections

John Owen is careful and clear to make sure we do not lose track of what he is unpacking here. Our minds are sometimes too logical and anchored in human reasoning. Spiritual aspects can escape us if there is no solid foundation to base everything on. So, he takes his time to outline how we become new spiritual beings through Jesus by using many verses from the Bible. These are not randomly dropped in but are meticulously re-

The Glory of Christ | 123

searched to build a case for what he is saying. It is good to have your Bible close by while reading and to look up certain verses that stand out to you. If you have time, read some of the context (the verses before and after) as this often makes the meaning clearer for us.

Owen is also clear when it comes to the Holy Spirit as part of the Godhead. Without his power and guidance, we cannot receive any of this wisdom and impartation that he is speaking of. It is good to ask the Holy Spirit to open your eyes and ears to understand exactly what is being said.

1. In the original version of this chapter, John Owen used the word "communication." In this modern version, we have substituted impartation and transmission in places to make it easier to understand. What is your understanding of this word?
2. What does he mean when he speaks about a "new creation"? Read 2 Corinthians 5:17.
3. How is Jesus' glory revealed through Christians? Do you see it in other believers? Do you think it shows in your life as a Christian?
4. What is the Holy Spirit's role in all of this?
5. What is this "new nature" that Owen talks about? Do you have it in you?

11

THE GLORY OF CHRIST IN RESTORATION

Lastly, Jesus is glorious in bringing all things together in him after they had been scattered and disordered by sin. Paul says this is the most powerful act of divine wisdom and the sovereign pleasure of God.

He lavished upon us, in all wisdom and insight making known to us the mystery of his will, according to his purpose, which he set forth in Christ as a plan for the fullness of time, to unite all things in him, things in heaven and things on earth. (Eph. 1:8–10)

An Outline of Redemption

To know the mind of the Holy Spirit in these words—to represent the glory of Jesus in them—we must quickly look at the origin of all these things in heaven and earth, their initial order, the confusion that followed, their restoration in Christ, and his glory as a result.

1. Only God has all being in him. That is why he gives himself the name, "I AM" (Exod. 3:14). He was eternally All. There was nothing else, and when there was, they were all "from him and through him and to him are all things" (Rom. 11:36). His being and goodness are the same. This is the first concept of the divine nature—infinite being and goodness existing in an intelligent and self-subsistent nature. The Bible says that "whoever would draw near to God must believe that he exists and that he rewards those who seek him" (Heb. 11:6).
2. In this state of infinite, eternal being and goodness, before his wisdom or power brought everything into existence, God was, and is, eternally in himself all that he will be, all that he can be, to eternity. For where there is infinite being and infinite goodness, there is infinite holiness and happiness, to which nothing can be added. God is always the same (Ps. 102:27). Nothing can add to God or change his state. His holiness, happiness, and self-satisfaction, as well as all other his infinite perfections, were absolutely the same before the creation of anything. There was nothing but himself: the indescribable mutual existence of the three holy persons in the same nature, with shared work of the Father and the Son in the eternal love and contentment of the Spirit. This gives us the true concept of the divine nature before it revealed itself through its power—infinite being and goodness, eternally blessed in the knowledge and enjoyment of itself by

inconceivable, mutual subsistence, which is in three distinct persons.

3. This goodness of God, by his own will and pleasure in infinite wisdom and power, created all things. From this, he made a finite, limited dependent being and goodness outside of himself. Since all being and goodness was in him, it was necessary that the first physical work and effect of the divine nature must be the impartation of being and goodness to other things. From nothing, by the word of his power, he said, "Let them be," and they were. And when he looked on all that he had made, he said "and behold, it was very good" (Gen. 1:31). Being and goodness must be the physical manifestation of the divine nature, which, worked by infinite power and wisdom, represents the glory of God in his creation.

4. In this state, all things that were made depended immediately on God himself without any other influence or rule. Their survival came from the divine nature that made them, and their dependence on God was by virtue of that law, rooted in the principles and powers of God's nature.

5. "In the beginning, God created the heavens and the earth." (Gen 1:1). He made two different groups that depend on him through obedience, and in so doing, give him glory. They live in two different places: heaven above and the earth beneath. The earth he gave to mankind to live on, suited to the survival and provision of its nature, to bring glory to God. Heaven, he

prepared for the angels, suitable for their nature and to give glory to God. While people had power and dominion over everything on the earth to use for the glory of God, the angels had similar dominion over the celestial and heavenly bodies, so God might receive glory and praise from them, too. To think there is another race of intellectual beings, besides angels in heaven and people on earth, is not only unsupported, but it disagrees with the order of the glory of God shown in the Bible, and the whole design of his wisdom and grace. Those thoughts are simply the fantasies of some people, without logic or wisdom.

6. This order of things was beautiful, which is why it was called "very good." Each of these groups had their own dependence on God. He was their immediate head, and there was no other between God and them. There was no impartation, except those directly from God himself. Even their own relationships with themselves were centered in God. So, he made the heavens and the earth, and two distinct groups in them, for himself.

7. This beautiful order, this union between the two groups, was disturbed, broken, and dissolved by the entrance of sin. Part of the family above, and the whole family below, fell off from their dependence on God. Without him as their head, there was dissension and hostility among themselves, because when the center of this union and order was removed and lost, only hatred and confusion remained. To show

that its goodness was lost, God cursed the earth and everything in it, for it was under man's dominion, which was now fallen from him. However, he did not curse the heavens, which were subject to the angels, because only some of them quit, so it was not cursed for those who stayed. But mankind was completely separated from God.

8. The angels that sinned were rejected by God forever as an example of his strictness. The whole race of mankind he would not completely throw off, but determined to recover and save a remnant, according to the election of grace.

9. However, he would not restore them to their previous position, to have two different groups again, each depending on him, even though he left them in different realms (Eph. 3:15). He would gather them both into one, under a new head, in whom the one part should be preserved from sinning and the other delivered from sin committed.

10. This is what Paul speaks of when he says, "to unite all things in him, things in heaven and things on earth," and "to reconcile to himself all things, whether on earth or in heaven" (Eph. 1:10, Col. 1:20). Everything fell into disorder and confusion through sin. They fell from God into conflict among themselves. God would not restore them to their previous position, depending on his divine perfections. He would no longer keep them in two separate families, but he would, in his wisdom and

goodness, bring them together under one head, on whom they should depend, and be reconciled again.
11. This new head that God has gathered up all things in heaven and earth into one, one body, one family, is Jesus Christ the Son of God incarnate. (1 Cor. 11:3, Eph. 1:22-23). This glory was reserved for him—no one else is worthy of it. (See Col. 1:17–19).
12. This new Head of God's reclaimed family was given all power in heaven and earth, all fullness of grace and glory to complete his role. There is no impartation from God, no act toward this family, no gift of power, grace, or goodness to angels or men, but what comes from the new head who holds them all. In him, they all consist, on him they depend, and to him they are subject. Their peace, union, and agreement among themselves are in him.
13. It is true that he acts differently toward the two parts of this reclaimed family of angels and men, according to their different states.
    a. We needed deliverance through redemption and grace, which the angels did not.
    b. Angels were capable of immediate confirmation in glory, which we are not until we come to heaven.

Therefore,

  a. Our nature might be repaired, not the nature of the angels.
    a. We have a relationship with him by his

Spirit, which exalts us to a place in the same family.

Jesus' Glory in Deliverance

After looking at this brief overview of this aspect of Jesus' glory, there are a few specifics worth pointing out.

No One Else Could

Only he was capable of doing this, bearing the weight of this glory. No being in heaven or earth was able to be made the head of the whole new creation of God. No one else could have all things depend upon him and be put in subjection to him, so there is no impartation between God and the creation but by and through him alone. So, when the Holy Spirit gives this glory to him, he is the only one who can fit this role, he is "the radiance of the glory of God and the exact imprint of his nature, and he upholds the universe by the word of his power" (Heb. 1:3),

The image of the invisible God, the firstborn of all creation. For by him, all things were created, in heaven and on earth, visible and invisible, whether thrones or dominions or rulers or authorities—all things were created through him and for him. And he is before all things, and in him all things hold together. (Col. 1:15–17)

Only he was able to bear and uphold this glory.

God Designed It for Him

This is the glory God designed for his only Son, and it gives us a view into the glory of that mystery, the wonderful eternal design of God to glorify himself in the incarnation of Christ. God would have his eternal, only-begotten Son to be incarnate, to take our nature on him—to be made man. What is his design in this incomprehensible work of wisdom, love, and power? It was for the redemption of the church, through his sacrifice and mediation. But there is more in this glory of God; that he might gather all things into one in him (Eph. 1:10). All creation, especially that which was to be eternally blessed, should have a new head to sustain, preserve, and bring order to it. All springs are in him, and all streams flow to him—in and by him to God. Who can express the divine beauty, order, and harmony of all things that are in Christ? The union and communion between angels and men—the order of heaven and earth; the transmission of life, grace, power, mercy, and comfort to the church; the rule and disposal of all things for the glory of God—depend on this. This glory God designed for his Son incarnate, and was the greatest, the highest that could be given to him. Paul says that all things are subject to him, and he is subject to one but God the Father (1 Cor. 15:27).

Thinking of the glory of Jesus should fill us with joy because he has brought everything together in him. One glimpse of him as God, as the supreme head of all creation, moving, acting, guiding, and disposing of it, will bring spiritual refreshment to the hearts of those who believe. More than that, it also gives a glorious representation of his divine nature. To think any other creature can be a head of life, motion, and power, and also rule over the new creation, is a foolish fantasy.

If we live more in thinking about this glory of Jesus, and of the wisdom of God in bringing all things in him, it would continually flow from our minds and actions.

He Restores

Jesus is glorious in repairing the whole divide that sin brought to the glory of God in the creation. The beauty and order of creation was in its dependence on God through the obedience of angels and men. The being, goodness, wisdom, and power of God were shown in this. But the beauty of this order was defaced, and the perfect glory of God was eclipsed by the entrance of sin. Now, everything is restored, repaired, and renewed in bringing it all under one new head: Christ Jesus. Divine creation is rendered more beautiful than it was before. That is why it groans for this restoration of all things. Whenever there is order, beauty, or glory, in heaven above or on earth below, it all comes from this new relation of creation to the Son of God. Whatever is not brought into one, in him, is in darkness, disorder, and under the curse. That is why the Jews have a saying, that "in the days of the Messiah all things shall be healed, but the serpent"—the devil, and wicked men, which are as his seed.

He Expresses God's Wisdom

He is glorious in being appointed as the only way all the treasures of the wisdom of God can be expressed toward his creatures. The wisdom of God is infinite. God does not, and cannot, act with more wisdom in one thing than in another—when he created man or other creatures. In the first creation, godly wisdom combined with infinite power: "O LORD, how manifold are your works! In wisdom have you made them all; the earth is full of your creatures" (Ps. 104:24). But when the effects of this divine wisdom, in their beauty and glory, were defaced, greater treasures of wisdom were required to restore them. And in reclaiming everything in Jesus, God used these to deal with his creatures. This is why Paul says, "that through the church the manifold wisdom of God might now be made known to the rulers and authorities in the heavenly places" (Eph. 3:10). By bringing everything under this one head, the unsearchable wisdom of God was revealed to the angels. They did not know before of God's design and work that would happen when sin entered. They could not comprehend the wisdom that would repair that loss. They did not know that divine wisdom had another way. But through the wisdom of God and all its treasures, working to achieve his glory, it becomes known to them. Divine wisdom revealed itself to angels and men. "In whom are hidden," and by him are displayed, "all the treasures of wisdom" (Col. 2:3). In this, he is glorious and will be for eternity.

He Is Our Security

He is glorious in the security expressed and given to the new creation. The first creation in its order was a unique and glorious thing until it was all lost through the sin of angels and men. But now, everything that belongs to this new creation, every believer in the world, as well as the angels in heaven, being gathered together in this one head, are safe from the destruction that fell on those before. In this new Head, we have an unshakable consistency.

Study Guide - Reflections

There was an old saying that "God don't make no junk." Despite what people see, you are made in God's image, and you are not rubbish, even though you may have fallen into the trash can and have started to look and smell like it. The good news is that God is in the restoration business! He is an expert at taking old, broken things that seem to be useless to others and shining them up really well so that they look almost better than they were. He knows how to renew, restore, revive, and repair us if we only allow him to do it. This is the good news of the Gospel. Jesus came to earth to restore us to himself.

It can be tough to hold onto this when we look in the mirror or get berated by our boss at work. One nasty remark from a friend or family member can send us reeling back to the trash can where we sit and mope for days and months. We think we deserve the bin—that we are not fit to be in God's presence. It's true: we're not unless Jesus restores us. He is the only one who can lift us up so his glory shines in his new creation.

1. In your own words, what does redemption mean? It might be good to use a few verses to back up your statements.
2. Why is Jesus the only one capable and able to deliver us?
3. Have you ever experienced this restoration and renewal in your own life? If not, perhaps speaking to someone you trust in the church

can really help you to understand where you're at.
4. Why do we need the wisdom of God? How is it different from normal wisdom? Read 1 Corinthians 1:25.
5. What does Owen mean when he says that we as Christians are safe from destruction?

12

DIFFERENCES BETWEEN FAITH AND SIGHT

We walk by faith, not by sight. —2 Cor. 5:7

In the life of God, our walking before him, and in our obedience, we are under the influence of faith, and not sight. Those are the two spiritual powers of our souls—by the one we can share in the grace, holiness, and obedience of this life; and by the other, we have eternal happiness and glory.

Both faith and sight—one in this life, the other in the life to come—have the same goal. They are the abilities of the soul to go forward and to embrace their object: the glory of Christ. But what is the difference between knowing the glory of Jesus in this world by faith, and the vision which we will have of the same glory in eternity?

The second forms part of Jesus' prayer for his disciples. "Father, I desire that they also, whom you have given me, may be with me where I am, to see my glory that you have given me" (John 17:24). But rather than looking at that, I want to focus on the work of God in this life, and the blessings that come from it. However, I will briefly outline the differences between faith and sight—the view we have of his glory in this world by faith, and that which those above enjoy with their eyes.

These differences can be under two categories:

1. Those that come from the different natures and actions in which we realize his glory: faith and vision.
2. Those that come from the different effects they produce.

Seeing Jesus by Faith

The view we have of the glory of Jesus by faith in this world is vague, hidden, and unclear. Paul says, "Now we see in a mirror dimly,"— "through" or by "a glass, in a riddle," a parable, an analogy (1 Cor. 13:12). There are two limitations to our view of this glory: seeing things and hearing words.

First, we do not have a clear view, more of a representation, as in a mirror—a reflection of what we cannot see. It is like seeing a person in a mirror, not their physical being, but only an imperfect image or representation.

The shadow or image of this glory of Jesus is shown in the Gospel as the likeness of a man. Even though it is obscure and imperfect compared to his real, substantial glory, which is seen in heaven, it is the only representation he has given us in this world. The cursed practice of making images of him out of sticks and stones or in paintings is so far from showing his real glory that it is not powerful enough to distract our thoughts from him. But Paul uses this figurative expression of seeing in a mirror to show the comparative imperfection of our present view of Jesus' glory.

We can extend this idea to a telescope, where we can see things far away. With this, people discover stars or comets that they are not able to see with their own eyes. And although it is not a perfect representation because of the distance, they see a full representation of it. The Gospel is a telescope that allows us to see his glory, but without it, we cannot discover Jesus.

Paul continues to describe this allusion used to reveal things to our minds, and it is through words. These are either plain and clear or dark, figurative, and in parables. This last method can make it difficult to understand perfectly, which is why our imperfect view of the glory of Christ by faith in this world, is in "a riddle." The Psalmist calls them "dark sayings" (Ps. 78:2).

But the description and representation of Jesus and his glory in the Gospel is not completely obscured and is also crystal clear, plain, and direct. Jesus is shown as crucified, exalted, and glorified. But Paul is not discussing the revelation of it to us, but of the method we use to understand that revelation. This is our faith, which is weak and imperfect, but allows us to comprehend the representation of this glory as we solve a riddle or understand a parable. It is not perfect and not always easy.

It is clear that we know so little of God, as Job reminds us (Job 24:14). How imperfect our concepts of him are! How weak our minds are in understanding! We cannot comprehend any of his glory in its fullness. What we do understand is in faith, although it is not a steady picture (Eph. 3:18). "For God, who said, 'Let light shine out of darkness,' has shone in our hearts to give the light of the knowledge of the glory of God in the face of Jesus Christ" (2 Cor. 4:6). God has revealed him to us, that we may love, admire, and obey him. But we are not able to constantly, steadily, and clearly behold his glory in this life, "for we walk by faith, not by sight" (2 Cor. 5:7).

Our sight of him here is like glimpses—clouded by many obstacles. "Behold, there he stands behind our wall, gazing through the windows, looking through the lattice" (Song. 2:9). There is a great barrier between him and us as a wall. Revealing himself to us, as through a window and lattice, means our view of him is imperfect. He is standing behind a wall that is between him and us. This wall is our present state, which must be demolished before we can see him as he is. In the meantime, he looks through the windows of the Gospel. When he wants to, he stands in those windows to show himself to us, but it is as imperfect as when we see someone through a window. His appearances are refreshing for us, but they are imperfect and temporary, leaving us to regret what we have lost. The best thing we can do then is to cry as the Psalmist did "As a deer pants for flowing streams, so pants my soul for you, O God. My soul thirsts for God, for the living God. When shall I come and appear before God?" (Ps. 42:1-2).

When will you give me another chance to see you, even if only through these windows? But Jesus goes further and displays himself through the lattices—by the promises of the Gospel. These are representations of the wonders and glories of Christ. How precious and wonderful he is in them! To see them fills our hearts to overflowing, even though it is through a lattice—unsteadily and unevenly.

The view of the glory of Jesus in this world is by faith. It is shadowed, weak, transient, imperfect, and partial. We can only discover it a little at a time, but in a short time, we will live in what we do discover. Sometimes, it is like the sun behind a cloud—we cannot perceive it. When he hides his face, who can see him? We can say what Job said:

Behold, I go forward, but he is not there, and backward, but I do not perceive him; on the left hand when he is working, I do not behold him; he turns to the right hand, but I do not see him. (Job 23:8-9)

Whichever way we turn, and whatever we do, we cannot see his glory fully. But sometimes it is like the sun shining brightly, and we cannot bear its rays. In infinite condescension he says to his church, "Turn away your eyes from me, for they overwhelm me" (Song. 6:5) —as if he could not bear the overwhelming affectionate love, which looks through the eyes of the church in its faith on him. Our souls are overwhelmed with his love when he clearly reveals his glory to us!

The Glory of Christ

Seeing Jesus With Our Eyes

Let us look at the vision we will have of the same glory in heaven, so we can compare these two.

Seeing the glory of Jesus in heaven is immediate, direct, and intuitive. Therefore, it is steady, even, and constant because of two things:

The Object We See

The object of it will be real and substantial. Jesus himself, in his own person, with all his glory, will be continually with us, before us. It is no longer an image, a representation of him, as we find in his glory in the Gospel. We will see him "face to face" (1 Cor. 13:12); "we shall see him as he is" (1 John 3:2)—not as we do now, an imperfect description of him. As a man sees his neighbor when they stand and talk together face-to-face, so we will see Jesus in his glory. It is not like Moses, who only had a transient glimpse of some parts of the glory of God when he passed by him.

Our eyes will see him as Job says: in our flesh, we will see our Redeemer and our eyes will behold him.

For I know that my Redeemer lives,

and at the last he will stand upon the earth.

And after my skin has been thus destroyed,

yet in my flesh I shall see God,

whom I shall see for myself,

and my eyes shall behold, and not another.

My heart faints within me! (Job 19:25-27)

What a joy that with the same eyes, we see the cup and bread of the communion and we will see him in person. This immediate vision is intellectual because it is not the human nature of Jesus, but his divine person and its nature that we see. In seeing the person of Christ, we will see a glory in it a thousand times more than we can conceive here on earth. Infinite wisdom, love, and power will be before us, and all the glories of the person of Jesus which we did not see so well before, will be vivid forever.

This is why it is a blessing to know "we will always be with the Lord" as he prays, that we would be with him and see his glory (1 Thess. 4:17, John 17:5). Here we have some shadowed views of it—we cannot see it perfectly until we are with him where he is. Then our view of him will be direct, intuitive, and constant.

There is a glory in us when we see this glory of Christ, which we cannot understand now because we do not know what we will become (1 John 3:2). Who can declare what glory it will be in us to see this glory of Jesus? And how excellent, then, is that glory of Jesus itself!

This immediate view of Christ is what all the saints of God in this life long for. That is why they are willing to die, or "desire... to depart and be with Christ," which is better (Phil. 1:23). They choose to "be away from the body and at home with the Lord" (2 Cor. 5:8), so they may enjoy the wonderful view of Jesus in his glory that they desire. Those who do not want it, whose souls and minds do not look for it, whose joy is worldly and blind, cannot see that far. Only those who are truly spiritual will be refreshed with these thoughts.

The Power We Receive

We will also be given the power to see the glory of Jesus. Without this, we cannot see him as he is. When he was transfigured on the mountain and had some reflections of his divine glory on his human nature, his disciples with him were more amazed than refreshed by it (Matt. 17:6). They saw his glory but spoke about it "not knowing" (Luke 9:30–33). The reason was that no one could have enough power, either spiritual or physical, to see Jesus' glory.

If Jesus appeared to any of us in his majesty and glory right now, it would not be for our edification or comfort. We are not capable, by the power of any light or grace we have received or can receive, to bear the immediate appearance and representation of them. John leaned on his chest many times, as one who loved him, but when Jesus later appeared to him in his glory, he "fell at his feet as though dead" (Rev. 1:17). And when he appeared to Paul, all that was said was he "saw on the way a light from heaven, brighter than the sun" and then fell "to the ground" (Acts 26:13-14).

This was one reason why, during his time on earth, his glory was hidden beneath the weakness of the flesh and many sufferings. The church today is not ready to commune with him in the immediate manifestations of his glory.

Therefore, those who dream of his personal reign on the earth before the day of judgment, unless they suppose that all the saints shall be perfectly glorified also, provide not at all for the edification or consolation of the church. For no grace we have now, no matter how great, can make us capable of conversing with Jesus in his revealed glory.

How foolish those people are who try to represent Jesus in his glory through pictures and images! A human eye will not just see their finest stained-glass windows but, with some logic, realize it is disgraceful and foolish. No inner or outer sight can bear the rays of Jesus' true glory in this life.

We are only capable of his presence with us by his Spirit. We do not know him in the flesh (2 Cor. 5:16). We are beyond knowing him through the rituals of the Old Testament, and we do not know him according to the physical presence that his disciples enjoyed. His ministry on earth meant that the promised gift of the Spirit could not be given until that was finished. Therefore, he tells his disciples that it is important that he leaves and sends the Spirit to them (John 16:7). Then they had a clearer view of the glory of Christ than when they saw him in the flesh. This is our spiritual attitude and condition. We are past the knowledge of him according to the flesh—we cannot physically see him in glory, but the life which we now lead is by the faith of the Son of God.

Without discussing the nature of this vision, or the power and ability we will have in heaven to see his glory, there are a few things that relate to our minds and bodies after the resurrection.

The Glory of Christ | 145

New Minds

The mind will be perfectly freed from all the darkness, unreliability, and other obstacles that weaken, hinder, and obstruct it in exercising our faith. There are types of hindrances:

The remains of our sinful, depraved natures. This causes our minds to become proud, dark, and corrupt, as the Bible mentions—unable to discern spiritual things. This is cured and removed by grace, so anyone in darkness becomes light in the Lord and can live for God with a new spiritual light given to them. But it is only partly removed, not completely abolished, so all we still have are our remaining weaknesses and obstacles in discerning things spiritual and eternal, which we yet groan under, and long to be delivered from. No footsteps, no scars, or marks that were in our minds will endure in glory (Eph. 5:27).

Nothing will weaken, disturb, or incapacitate our souls in all their powers; they will be unrestricted by pride, distractions, or weakness to be able to reach their proper objects. The greatness of freedom and power is inconceivable. We cannot imagine the glory and beauty of the spiritual actions of our minds without being blocked or having any rubbish in them. One pure act of spiritual sight in discerning the glory of Jesus—one pure act of love in embracing God—will bring more happiness and satisfaction to our minds than we are capable of in this world.

Our earthly minds are incapable of spiritual and eternal things, and this is natural because of where we are.

They are made of flesh which is polluted and corrupted. In this state, the mind acts its ideas through the body as its instrument and is stuck in this prison of the flesh. There is a spiritual excellence in the pure actions of the soul when delivered from all earthly instruments, or when they are all glorified and made suitable for spiritual things. How our minds will be freed from these obstructions to see the glory of Jesus will be looked at later.

A new light, the light of glory, will be embedded in them. There is a light in nature, which is the power of a person to discern natural things—an ability to know, perceive, and judge. It is that "spirit of man" which "is the lamp of the LORD, searching all his innermost parts" (Prov. 20:27).

But by its light, no one can discern spiritual things (1 Cor. 2:11–15). That is why God gives a superior, supernatural light—the light of faith and grace—to those he calls to the knowledge of himself by Jesus Christ. He shines into their hearts to give them the knowledge of his glory in the face of his dear Son. Although this new light does not abolish or blot out the other light of nature, just as the rising sun causes the light of the stars to fade, it directs it to its main object and goal. Anyone that only has the natural light cannot understand anything of it, because they have no taste or experience of its power and work. They might speak and ask about it, but they do not know it.

We have received this light of faith and grace that lets us discern spiritual things and see the glory of Jesus imperfectly. But in heaven there will be an extra light of glory, which will make our minds "shine like the brightness of the sky above" (Dan. 12:3). There are three things to say about this:

1. The light of grace does not destroy or abolish the light of nature but rectifies and improves it. The light of glory will not abolish or destroy the light of faith and grace but combine with it to make it completely perfect.
2. The light of nature does not allow us to clearly comprehend the true nature and power of the light of grace, because it is not the same and is seen only in its own light. But the light of grace does not allow us to comprehend this light of glory, since it is different, only seen perfectly by its own light.
3. This is the best perception we can have of this light of glory: that it perfectly transforms the soul into the image and likeness of Christ.

This is how our nature progresses to its rest and happiness. The principles remaining in it concerning good and evil, with its practical convictions, are not destroyed but improved by grace. The blindness, darkness, and hostility to God are partly taken away. Being renewed by grace, what it receives here of spiritual life and light will never be destroyed but be perfected in glory. Grace renews nature, glory perfects grace, and the soul is brought to rest in God. We see it in the blind man our Savior healed (Mark 8:22–24). He was born completely blind. At the first touch, his eyes were opened, and he saw, but very vaguely—he saw men walking like trees. But the second time, he saw everything clearly. Our minds are also blind. The first touch by grace gives them a view of spiritual, heavenly, and eternal things, although it is obscure and unsteady. The sight of glory makes everything clear and evident.

New Bodies

The body as glorified, with its senses, shall have its use and peace herein. After we are clothed again with our flesh, we will see our Redeemer with our eyes. We do not know now what power and spirituality will be in our glorified bodies, but they will be part of our eternal happiness. Stephen, the first martyr, experienced glory by anticipation before he died. When he was brought to his trial, everyone "gazing at him... saw that his face was like the face of an angel" (Acts 6:15). He had his own transfiguration, similar to that of our Savior on the mountain. By this initial beam of glory, he received such energy and edge to his physical eyes, that despite the distance between the earth and heaven, he looked up and "saw the glory of God, and Jesus standing at the right hand of God" (Acts 7:55-56). Who can say what power this sense of sight will have when perfectly glorified or what wonderful refreshing will come to our souls because of it?

It was a privilege to have physically seen Him as his disciples did when he was on the earth as he says, "For truly, I say to you, many prophets and righteous people longed to see what you see" (Matt. 13:17). If it was such a privilege for them, then how wonderful and glorious it will be, when our own eyes, gloriously purified and strengthened beyond those of Stephen, will see

Jesus in the fullness of his glory! Only he understands this, because he prayed to his Father that those who believe in him may be where he is, to see his glory.

A Future Hope

The difference between seeing his glory by faith here and seeing it in heaven is that the one is weak, imperfect, and obscure, while the other is direct, immediate, and constant.

This view is what we are longing and panting for, what Jesus prays for us to have, and what the apostle claims is best: that which brings eternal rest and satisfaction to our souls.

On earth, our souls are burdened with many weaknesses, and our faith is obstructed through ignorance and darkness. Our best efforts are with groans for deliverance: "But we ourselves, who have the first fruits of the Spirit, groan inwardly as we wait eagerly for adoption as sons, the redemption of our bodies" (Rom. 8:23). While we are in this physical temple, we groan and are burdened, because we are not "away from the body and at home with the Lord" (2 Cor. 5:2-8). The more we grow in faith and spiritual light, the more aware we are of our present burdens, and the more passionately we groan for deliverance into the perfect freedom of the sons of God. This is the attitude of those who have received the first fruit of the Spirit in the highest degree. The nearer we are to heaven, the more we desire to be there, because Jesus is there. The more frequent and focused our views are of him by faith, the more we long and groan for all the obstructions to be removed. Groaning is the passionate expression of desire, mixed with sorrow. The desire has sorrow, and that sorrow has joy and refreshment in it— like rain that falls on a person in a garden in the spring; he gets wet but is not refreshed the same way the flowers are. Constant and habitual groaning is one of the best results of faith in this life— it respects what we want to be delivered from, and what we want to achieve (Rom. 7:24). This groaning, mixed with sighs of weariness from the troubles, sorrows, pains, sicknesses of this life, is the best we can here manage here on earth.

Unfortunately, we cannot think of Jesus without becoming ashamed of our own thoughts that are so confused, unsteady, and imperfect. We often groan and sigh at these: Oh, when will we be with him? When will we see him as he is? When he gives us more than the normal expressions of his glory and love to our hearts, we cannot bear them, for they are too much for our minds. But usually, this trouble and groaning is one of the best we can have in this world—a trouble I pray never to be delivered from until deliverance comes to my mortal body. Lord, increase this trouble more and more in everyone who believes.

Set on Jesus

The heart of a believer affected by the glory of Jesus is like the needle touched with a magnet. It cannot remain quiet or be satisfied when it is far from him. It is set in continual motion toward him. This motion is weak and unsteady, with much sighing and groaning in prayer, in meditations, in the secret corners of our minds. However, it is continually pressing towards him, even though it never reaches its goal: it never comes to its center and rest, in this world.

In heaven, all things are clear and peaceful—evident in seeing the glory of Jesus—we will be with him forever and see him as he is. This is heaven, happiness, and eternal rest.

The person of Jesus in all his glory will always be before us, and the eyes of our understanding will be gloriously illuminated, so that we can steadily see and comprehend that glory.

But on earth, our minds withdraw, our meditations fail, our hearts are overcome, our thoughts confused, and our eyes turn away from the brilliance of this glory. We cannot remain long thinking about it. But in heaven, an immediate, constant view of it will bring everlasting refreshing and joy to our souls.

Seeing the glory of Jesus given to him by his Father is inferior to the ultimate vision of the essence of God. That, we cannot properly conceive, except that we know the pure in heart will see God (Matt. 5:8) But it is connected, and without it, we can never see the face of God as our soul's intended happiness. For he is, and will be for eternity, the only communication between God and the church.

There are some guidelines for looking into and longing after this perfect view of Jesus' glory that we find in the Old Testament. The sight they had of the glory of Christ—they also saw his glory through the obscurity of its revelation, although veiled—was weak and imperfect in the most illuminated believers. It was inferior to what we now have by faith, through the Gospel. Yet it was as still an encouragement for them to ask and search after what was being revealed (1 Peter 1:10-11). However, their discoveries were dim and confused, as people see things in the distance (Isa. 33:17). The continuation of this veil on his glory—their hearts and minds were ignorant and blind—caused many to fall away (2 Cor. 3:7-14). This double veil (the covering covered, the veil veiled) God promised to take away (Isa. 25:7) and then they will turn to the Lord when they can clearly see the glory of Christ (2 Cor. 3:16).

Desiring to See More

But this caused those who were real believers among them to desire, long, and pray for the removal of these veils and shadows, that were like night compared to "the sun of righteousness [that] shall rise with healing in its wings" (Mal. 4:2). For them, "the day breathes and the shadows flee" (Song. 2:17, 4:6). Paul uses the analogy of giving birth when explaining this desire and expectation of the Son of God being revealed in the flesh, and all promises that come with it (Rom. 8:19). That is why he was called the Lord whom they sought and delighted in (Mal. 3:1).

The believers in those days had great spiritual wisdom, rejoicing in the rituals of worship. They saw them as a privilege, diligently performing them as a result of divine wisdom and love, and also because they were an indication of good things to come. At the same time, they longed and desired for the time of reformation, where all of it would be removed so they could see and enjoy the good things they represented. Those who chose to rather trust their own traditions were not accepted by God, but those who were enlightened lived in constant desire for the revelation of the whole mystery of the wisdom of God in Jesus, just as the angels did (1 Peter 1:3, Eph. 3:9-10).

With this attitude of heart, they had more of the power of true faith and love than we see in many Christians today. They saw the promises from far away, were convinced of them, and embraced them (Heb. 11:13). They reached out to embrace the things that were promised. We see this in old Simeon, who took baby Jesus in his arms and cried out for God to let "your servant depart in peace" (Luke 2:28-29). Let me die for I have seen what my soul has longed for!

Our current darkness and weakness in seeing the glory of Jesus is not like theirs. It is not because of a veil shrouded in rituals and emblems, and it does not come from the lack of a clear doctrinal revelation of who Jesus is, but from two other causes.

- First, the nature of faith compared to sight. It is not able to look directly into this excellent glory or comprehend it completely.
- Secondly, the way it is revealed is not complete but only an image of it, as in a mirror.

The view of his glory we will have in heaven is more than what we enjoy through the Gospel, and what we enjoy now is more than what they had through their rituals and representations. The distance between the vision of heaven and the sight which we have now by faith is far bigger than the one between the sight we have now and the one they had under the Old Testament. Heaven surpasses the Gospel more than that state surpasses the Law. If they prayed, longed for, and desired the removal of their shadows and veils to be able to see what we see now, that they might see the glory of Jesus as we see it through the Gospel, how much more should we, if we have the same faith and love, long and pray for the removal of all weakness, darkness, and obstacles, so we can see his glory the way Jesus prayed we would see it!

A Brief Summary

There are three things concerning the glory of Jesus, three degrees in its manifestation—the shadow, the perfect image, and the real thing. Those in the Old Testament only had a shadow of it, and of the things that belong to it—they did not have the perfect image of them (Heb. 10:1). In the Gospel, we have the perfect image, which they did not. It is a clear, complete revelation and declaration of it, shown to us as in a mirror. But the enjoyment of these things is reserved for heaven—we must be where he is, that we may see his glory. There is a greater difference and distance between the real thing and the most perfect image of it, than there is between the most perfect image and the shadow of the same thing. So, if they longed to be free from all the shadows, to enjoy the representation of the glory of Jesus in the way he is shown in the Gospel, how much more should we long and pant to be delivered from seeing only an image of it, to enjoy the real thing. Whatever is revealed of Jesus on this side of heaven, it is so we may passionately desire to be present with him even more.

They had wisdom and grace to rejoice in the light and rituals of divine worship which eclipsed the glory of Jesus from them, yet they always longed for the better light and full discovery of it in the Gospel. And it will also be ours to use and improve the revelations that we enjoy, and those institutions of worship that assist our faith—to continually breathe after that perfect, glorifying sight reserved for heaven above.

Should we not examine ourselves in this regard? Is pressing in toward the perfect view of Jesus' glory our duty? Do we engage in it? If the answer is no, it is a sign that we are hypocrites. If Jesus is in us, he is the hope of glory in us. Wherever that hope is, it will be active in desiring the things we hope for. Many people love the world too much, and their minds are too full of it, entertaining thoughts of quickly seeing the glory of Jesus. They are at home, unwilling to be with the Lord. They hope that the time for heaven will come later when they have had their full of earth. But their view of his glory in this world by faith is small if any at all—they do not wish to see Jesus face-to-face. I cannot understand how any person can walk with God or love Jesus in true faith, or find satisfaction and joy in spiritual things, if they do not meditate on the glory of Jesus in heaven every chance they get, longing to see him.

Only Jesus understood what the eternal happiness of those who believe in him consisted of. This is what he prayed for—that we may be where he is, to see his glory. It is our duty to continuously desire what he prayed for so we may attain it.

To those who are conditioned to think about these things, they are salt for their lives, where everything becomes savory. A lack of spiritual diligence has resulted in a negligent, careless, worldly religion, filled with rituals that have no power of faith and love in them. Many deceive themselves this way. Goods, lands, possessions, relationships, and businesses are the images drawn in their minds, and the characters are written on their foreheads—the titles they are known by. As believers, seeing the glory of Jesus in the mirror of the Gospel, we are changed into the image and likeness of the Lord by the Spirit. But those who see the beauty of the world in the cursed mirror of self-love are changed into the same image in their minds. That is why strange fears, useless hopes, empty embraces of fading things, fruitless desires, earthly, carnal designs, cursed, self-pleasing imaginations, feeding on, and being fed by, the love of the world and self, live in them. But we have learned a different way in Jesus.

Study Guide - Reflections

Our Christian walk is all based on faith. While we know there is incredible strength in this virtue, it can also be a frustrating part of being a Christian. We struggle to see the wood for the trees in our own lives, so how are we expected to see his glory? No wonder atheists laugh at the notion of believing something invisible and mock us for not using our own brains and logic! Faith can be hard to define, difficult to find, and impossible to measure at times. Jesus said that we only have to have faith the size of a mustard seed to remove mountains, but in the next moment, we fall flat because we are the ones who only have "little faith!" (Matt. 8:26).

Owen says that we need faith if we want to maintain our spiritual life, grow in Jesus, and see any of his glory this side of heaven. He explains the difference between the here and now, and the hereafter. He also shows why, as much as we want to, we cannot see his full glory here on earth. We are not capable of this view. And so, we see shadows of it, hints and parts. But we need to exercise our faith to hold onto these glimpses, as they will carry us to the end.

1. If you had to rate your faith out of 10, what score would you give yourself?
2. What aspect of faith do you struggle with the most?
3. What is the difference between faith and sight? Why does this difference exist?
4. What gave the believers in the Old Testament faith to continue, faith that Owen says is more than "we see in many Christians today"?
5. Owen describes those who have been touched by Jesus' glory as magnetized needles—they are never satisfied or still unless they point toward him, longing to see him. Do you have this longing, this pull, this desire in you?

13

OBSTACLES TO SEEING THE GLORY OF CHRIST

Faith is the light through which we see the glory of Jesus in this world. In itself, it is weak and imperfect, like weak eyes that cannot see the sun in its full beauty. That is why our view of it differs greatly from what we will enjoy in heaven. But it is also often hindered and interrupted in its work, or it loses the view of its object one way or another. The person who sees anything from far, sees it imperfectly, and the slightest interference or movement makes him lose sight. It is the same with our faith—sometimes we can have a little view and sometimes no sight at all of his glory by it. This is another difference between faith and direct sight.

Although this seems like we are going off the point, I insist on showing the reasons why many have hardly any experience in the things we have spoken about—they find so little of reality or power in this duty. The defect is in themselves.

The Imperfection of Faith

While we are in this life, Jesus is pleased, in his wisdom, to sometimes withdraw and 'hide' from us. Then our minds are clouded with darkness, faith is unsure, and we cannot see his glory—we seek him but cannot find him. So, Job complains, "Behold, I go forward, but he is not there, and backward, but I do not perceive him; on the left hand when he is working, I do not behold him; he turns to the right hand, but I do not see him," (Job 23: 8-9). Whichever way I turn, whatever I do, in whatever manner I seek him, I cannot find him, I cannot see him—I cannot behold his glory. So, the church also complains, "Truly, you are a God who hides himself, O God of Israel, the Savior" (Isa. 45:15), and the Psalmist cries, "How long, O Lord? Will you hide yourself forever?" (Ps. 89:46). God hiding his face is hiding the light of his glory in the face of Jesus, and therefore, of the glory of Jesus himself, because it is the glory of Jesus to be the representative of the glory of God. The spouse in Song of Songs is often at a loss, and complains that her Beloved has hidden, that she could not find or see him (Song. 3:1- 2, 6).

People can hold onto their ideas about Jesus, his person and his glory. These cannot be blotted out of their minds except through heresy or stupidity. They can have the same doctrinal knowledge of him, but the sight of his glory is not there. They can keep all the rituals and practices he commands, but when it comes to imparting himself into their hearts or having a wonderful refreshing view of his glory, he withdraws and hides himself from them.

In the New Testament, he reveals himself to some, and not to others—"How is it that you will manifest yourself to us, and not to the world?" (John 14:22),—those he shows himself to see him as beautiful, glorious, and lovely, while the others see nothing, and wonder how they admire him so much (Song. 5:9). Sometimes he hides his face, turns away the light of his countenance, clouds the rays of his glory to some, while others are warmed by them.

We must ask two questions here:

1. Why does Jesus hide himself in his glory from the faith of believers, that they cannot see him?
2. How can we know when he withdraws himself from us so that whatever we do, we will not see his glory?

Why He Hides

It is an act of sovereign, unaccountable wisdom. One of the reasons he does this is to stir us up to diligently search and inquire after him. Laziness and carelessness often hinder our meditations on heavenly things. Even though our hearts are awake (as the spouse speaks in Song. 5:2) to consider Christ, his love, and his grace, we are asleep in exercising our faith and love toward him. Who can justify themselves in this? Who can say, "My heart is pure, I am clean from this sin?" He must be praised for his patience, that even in our unkindness and negligence, he has withdrawn himself for a season, but not completely departed from us. For those who see his glory and enjoy his presence, even though they have not valued the mercy and privilege of it as they should, they cannot bear his absence or hide himself from them. This way, he will wake them up to diligently inquire after him. When they find he is absent and his glory is so far from them that their faith cannot reach it, they become like the doves of the valleys, mourning their iniquity, not motivating themselves to seek him (Hosea 5:15). So, whatever reason the spouse gives for Jesus withdrawing from her, she immediately gives an account of her restless diligence and efforts to ask after him until she has found him (Song. 3:1–4; 5:2–8). In this search, faith and love are exercised; even though it is in sighs and groans, it is acceptable and pleasing to him.

We are like the person in the parable of the prophet who spoke to Ahab, who had to look after one thing, but because he was busy here and there, that one disappeared. Jesus commits himself to us, and we should carefully keep his presence. "I held him," says the church, "and would not let him go" (Song. 3:4). But while we are busy here and there, while our minds are consumed with other things, he withdraws himself—we cannot find him. But even this rebuke is for our recovery, and his return to us.

I speak to those whose acts of faith and love in and toward Jesus is their main priority, in their whole walk before God.

The first thing to see is the consequences of his withdrawal. We can only know these through the effects of his presence with us, and the manifestation of himself to us—in these times, this will cease. The life, energy, and grace in us is an inseparable consequence and effect of seeing his glory. While we enjoy it, we live—Christ lives in us, working in us.

Paul says that while "beholding the glory of the Lord, [we] are being transformed into the same image from one degree of glory to another," (2 Cor. 3:18). Through faith we think on Jesus' glory as revealed in the Gospel, then grace grows and works in us toward a perfect conformity to him. While we remain in this view, our souls are in a holy attitude and in a continuous exercise of love and joy. It is impossible for us to see Jesus in faith and not want to be more like him and love him. And we cannot do these unless we have a constant view of him and his glory by faith, which powerfully works in us. All the doctrinal knowledge we have of him is useless; all the views of his glory are fantasy or superstition unless they are accompanied by this transforming power. From this power, we have an increase and energy of grace, because that is where our conformity to him exists. Growth in grace, holiness, and obedience is growing closer to Christ, nothing else.

Replaced by Idols

This transforming power from spiritually seeing Jesus is not in the minds of those who are carnal and ignorant of the mystery of believing. They have exchanged it for fantasies and superstitions. Crucifixes and images with paintings represent him in his sufferings and glory. Through these, their emotions are stimulated through physical senses, and they think they are affected by him and are close to him. Some have even started making wounds on their hands, feet, and sides, pretending to be like him, to be transformed into his image. But whatever is produced by an image is just an image. An imaginary Jesus will bring nothing in people's minds but imaginary grace.

In this, faith has been lost and died. When men could not find any experience in their minds of the spiritual mysteries of the Gospel or feel any spiritual change or blessing through them, they substituted some rituals in their place. These produced some sort of effect on their minds and emotions, but a different nature than the real effects of true evangelical grace.

Everyone agrees that seeing Jesus Christ and his glory will make us love him and make us become more like him. But religious churches say this is done by looking at crucifixes with other images and pictures of him, while we see his glory by faith, as revealed in the Gospel, and no other way. Some reject using images, but they also despise the spiritual view of glory. These people will fall on the other side because anything is better than nothing.

We have a clear prophecy prohibiting such images, so then a spiritual view of Jesus to transform us into his own likeness is necessary. Those images leave impressions on people's minds, partly because their senses and imaginations are easily triggered by their thoughts, and partly from their natural inclinations to superstition, being averse to spiritual and invisible things and opting for things that are present and visible. They think it is with a love for Jesus.

These things serve no other purpose than to divert people's minds from faith and love for Jesus, giving them satisfaction as their emotions cling to their idols. We need the wisdom of faith and spiritual light to discern and judge between the effects of natural emotions toward spiritual objects—wrong motives with wrong goals.

But there is a real experience of power in spiritually seeing the glory of Jesus by faith, as proposed in the Gospel, to strengthen, increase, and motivate individuals to proper duties, changing and transforming the soul gradually into his likeness, which keeps us from all those hypocritical practices.

How We Know He Has Withdrawn

Here we can understand why the Lord withdraws himself so we cannot see his glory, even though we search for it. If we grow weak in our Christian character, unspiritual in our attitudes, cold in our emotions, or careless in meditation, it is clear that he is far from us, so we do not see his glory as we should. When the weather grows cold, plants wither, and frost appears on the ground; everyone knows the sun has left and does not show itself. If it is the same with our hearts, that we grow cold, frozen, withering, lifeless, in our spiritual duties, then Jesus has withdrawn in some way, and we will not see his glory. We still have the truth about him, but faith is not strong enough to see him and his glory. There is nothing more certain in Christianity than this is: while we see his glory by faith—his person and role—and remain in holy thoughts and meditations of it, all grace will live and flourish in us, especially with love for him and all that belongs to him. If we put it to the test, we will always find the promised result.

Do we experience a decline in grace: deadness, coldness, lukewarmness, a kind of spiritual senselessness? Do we find a hesitation to engage in our duties toward God? Do we want our souls to be saved from these dangerous diseases? There is no better way for our healing and deliverance than a fresh view of the glory of Christ by faith and remaining there.

Some say this comes from a fresh pouring out of the Holy Spirit. Unless he falls like dew and rain on our dry and barren hearts; unless he causes our Christian characters to spring, thrive, and bear fruit; unless he revives and increases faith, love, and holiness in our souls, our backsliding will not be healed, and our spiritual state will not recover. This is what was prayed for and promised in the Bible (Song. 4:16, Isa. 44:3, 4, Ezek. 11:19, Ezek. 36:26, Hos. 14:5-6). The immediate power of reviving our souls is from and by the Holy Spirit. But how do we get this? Through seeing the glory of Christ in a mirror, we "are being transformed into the same image from one degree of glory to another." It is in the exercise of faith in Jesus that the Holy Spirit brings his renewing, transforming power in and on our souls. This is the only way Christians will recover from their backsliding and deadness.

Some complain about their state. Those who are dead and dull do not know if there is any spark of heavenly life left in them. Some make weak efforts at recovery, as if in a dream where they make great attempts without any success. Some get involved in many duties and services. Most just whine in their careless condition. The reason is that they will not sincerely and constantly use the only cure and relief. It is like a person who chooses to suffer in sickness with useless, temporary treatments rather than use a known and approved remedy because using it does not suit their lifestyle. But Jesus tells us how to live in the exercise of faith in him:

Abide in me, and I in you. As the branch cannot bear fruit by itself, unless it abides in the vine, neither can you, unless you abide in me. I am the vine; you are the branches. Whoever abides in me and I in him, he it is that bears much fruit, for apart from me you can do nothing. (John 15:4-5)

There is a double reason to come to Jesus by believing. The first is that we may have life—a spring and principle of spiritual life imparted to us from him, because he is "[our] life" (Col. 3:4), and "because [he] lives, [we] also will live" (John 14:19). It is not so much we that live, as he lives in us (Gal. 2:19-20). There is unbelief when we want life but do not come to him (John 5:40). Secondly, believers come to him in faith, that they may "have life and have it abundantly" (John 10:10), as well as grace to keep their souls in a healthy, energetic work of the power of spiritual life. As he rebukes those who will not come to him to receive life, so he rebukes us all, for we do not come to him in faith to have this life more abundantly.

When Jesus is near us and we see his glory, he will often refresh us with peace, consolation, and joy in our hearts. This not only energizes our Christian characters, but we are aware of him imparting himself and his love to us. When the Sun of Righteousness rises on the soul, it will find "healing in its wings" (Mal. 4:2)—his beams of grace carry spiritual refreshment by his Spirit.

He is present with us by his Spirit, and these are his fruits and effects—he is the Comforter promised to us.

Many people live a very careless, unwise Christianity. As long as they carry on performing the external rituals, they have no idea of the greatest evangelical blessings—the marrow of divine promises, the real efforts of a vital relationship with Jesus. Spiritual peace, refreshing comfort, indescribable joy, and the composure of assurance. Without a taste and experience of these, being a Christian is heartless, lifeless, and useless—religion is a dead carcass without a living soul.

The peace some have is from their own foolishness. They do not see these as the substance of Jesus' reward, and that rejecting them would actually deprive the church of its main support and encouragement in times of suffering. It is evidence of how powerful unbelief is when we can satisfy ourselves without experiencing these things in our hearts—the joy, peace, consolation, and assurance promised in the Gospels. How can we believe the promises of things for the future—heaven, immortality, and glory—when we do not believe the promises of the present reward in these spiritual privileges? How will we believe them, when we do not attempt to have an experience of them in our hearts, to be content without them? People deceive themselves this way. They want spiritual joy, peace, and assurance to mask their evil attitudes and careless living. Some have attempted to have both at the same time, to the ruin of their souls. Without the diligent exercise of obedience, we will never enjoy the grace of comfort.

In seeing the glory of Jesus as he comes to us and abides with us, we have spiritual peace, consolation, joy, and assurances. These are a part of the royal robe of his graces, of his reward with him (Rev, 22:12). Wherever he is with someone, these things are never lacking, unless it is their own fault or to test them. This is how he shows his love to the church (Song. 7:12). "And he who loves me will be loved by my Father, and I will love him and manifest myself to him... my Father will love him, and we will come to him and make our home with him" (John 14:21, 23) and "eat with him" (Rev. 3:20), which is an impartation of those spiritual refreshments.

How do we receive them? It is in seeing the glory of Jesus by faith (1 Peter 1:8-9). It is the glory of his person, his role, his condescension, exaltation, love, and grace. Faith must fix itself on this in sight and thought, mix itself with it, meditate on it, and embrace it, then Jesus will bring spiritual, supernatural refreshment and joy to our souls. With faith to discover the glory of Jesus, we should not lack these hints of his love, the outpouring of it in his heart, like a living fountain of spiritual refreshments (John 4:14, Rom. 5:5).

Those Who Object

Some people claim this is all fiction; they renounce the Gospel, the powers of the world to come, and the whole work of the Holy Spirit as the comforter. All relationship between Jesus believers' hearts is completely overthrown, reducing all religion to an external show, a display that belongs on a stage rather than in the temple of God—our minds. According to them, there is no such thing as the pouring out of the love of

God in our hearts by the Holy Spirit, or the Spirit of God witnessing with our spirits that we are the children of God, which brings us joy and refreshment. To them, there is no such thing as God shining his face on us, bringing joy to our hearts; no such thing as rejoicing or "believing, with joy unspeakable and full of glory;" no such thing as Jesus showing himself to us, eating with us, and giving us his love. There are no divine promises of a "feast of rich food, a feast of well-aged wine" in gospel mercies (Isa. 25:6). They claim that all those celebrations in the spirit that many faithful martyrs enjoyed when they saw the glory of God in Jesus, that they testified about in their last moments, were nothing but fiction. But these irreverent mockers have the audacity to proclaim their own ignorance of those things which are the real powers of what we believe.

There are others who will not deny the truth of these things or contradict those who use the Bible to confirm them. They assume some people participate in them, but they have no experience of it all, nor is it something they think they should strive after. They can make a shift to live in hopes of heaven and future glory, but when it comes to now, they desire nothing more except to do what they are convicted to do—this gives them a sorry peace which they enjoy. So, many tolerate their spiritual apathy and unbelief, being free to look for refreshment and satisfaction in other things without despising the Gospel. All these things are inconsistent. When people look for refreshment and satisfaction in temporary things, it is impossible for them to seek after those things that are spiritual. When we have tasted spiritual comforts and joys, our desire and satisfaction in current pleasures will fade (Phil. 3:8-9).

Faith in Christ

But the truth is that when Jesus is present with us—not withdrawn for a season, living in the view of his glory by faith—he will give us touches of his love, supplies of his Spirit, joy and rejoicing, and rest in assurance, to refresh our souls, fill us with joy, satisfy us with spiritual delight, and motivate us to a closer relationship with himself.

Let us not dishonor the Gospel. Knowing that our faith and obedience are often accompanied by physical troubles, afflictions, persecution, and criticisms, as we were warned, we cannot say that the inner relief and divine refreshment we experience does not outweigh all those evils that we may go through upon the account of the Gospel. To think this way is contrary to the promise of Jesus who assured us that "in this time," in this world, we will receive a reward a hundred times more than everything we lose or suffer for his sake (Mark 10:30). It is the same for those who "joyfully accepted the plundering of your property," as they will have "a better possession and an abiding one" in heaven (Heb. 10:34). If we do not participate in these things and are strangers to them, the blame is ours alone.

The reason for Jesus withdrawing himself from us and hiding his glory from our view is to build our grace, to motivate us to diligently ask after him. This is where we find our guidance and direction. Do we find ourselves lifeless in the spiritual duties of Christianity? Are we strangers to the spiritual gifts of comfort and joy—those visitations of God in which he preserves our souls? Do we seldom enjoy a sense of the "love... poured into our hearts through the Holy Spirit?" (Rom. 5:5). We have no way of recovery except in this: we must turn to this "strong tower" as "prisoners of hope" and look to Jesus that we may be saved. A constant view and contemplation of his glory by faith will bring all these to our hearts and souls.

Obstacles to Faith

If we lose sight of his glory and our faith is hindered, it can be our fault because all our spiritual disadvantages come from ourselves. The lusts and corruptions we still have, indulged by laziness and negligence or excited and inflamed by Satan's temptations, obstruct us. Whilst they are in any disorder or disturbance, it is in vain for us to expect any clear view of this glory.

The view of Jesus' glory we speak of consists of two things: its special nature, and its necessary effect. The first is a spiritual perception or understanding as it is revealed in the Bible. The revelation of the glory of his person, role, and grace is the main subject of the Bible and the main object of our faith. The other consists of different thoughts about him, acting in faith, in love, trust, delight, and longing after the full enjoyment of him (1 Peter 1:8).

If we satisfy ourselves in ideas and speculations about this glory as it is doctrinally revealed, we will find no transforming power in it. But, in a spiritual light, we are drawn to him with full purpose of heart, our minds are filled with thoughts of him and delight in him, and our faith is constantly focused on trust in him. Righteousness will come from him to purify our hearts, increase our holiness, strengthen our character, and fill us "with joy unspeakable and full of glory." This is the right temperature for spiritual health—when our knowledge of the glory of God in Jesus answers our desires, and our longing for Jesus is in line with that light. Where the light leaves the emotions and desires behind, it ends in formality or atheism, and where emotions outrun light, they sink into the bog of superstition, adoring images and pictures. But to avoid this excess, it is better that our emotions exceed our light from the defect of our understandings than that our light exceed our emotions from the corruption of our wills. In both, faith is often interrupted and obstructed by the corruption still in us, especially if it is not constantly kept under the discipline of humility.

Sin Clouds Understanding

For those who do not, the steam of their disorder clouds and darkens their understanding, so it is not possible to clearly discern anything spiritual. There is nothing worse, naturally and morally than the chaos of passions and emotions that blind, darken, and deceive the mind. It is it is more harmful in the spirit, where that confusion becomes a rebellion against the pure light—the light and rule of grace.

There are three kinds of people whose view is obstructed when the Gospel is preached.

1. **Stubborn unbelievers.** The power of Satan on stubborn unbelievers' minds blinds them,

making it impossible to see anything of Jesus' glory. Paul says that

even if our gospel is veiled, it is veiled to those who are perishing. In their case the god of this world has blinded the minds of the unbelievers, to keep them from seeing the light of the gospel of the glory of Christ, who is the image of God." (2 Cor. 4:3-4)

We are not talking about these people here.

2. **Lovers of the world.** We all have a corrupt, natural darkness in us, a depravity in our minds that stops us from seeing this glory. So, "the light shines in the darkness, and the darkness has not overcome it" (John 1:5). For "the natural person does not accept the things of the Spirit of God, for they are folly to him, and he is not able to understand them because they are spiritually discerned" (1 Cor. 2:14). Even though Jesus is preached to us, only a few discern any glory or beauty in him for which he should be desired, as the prophet complains (Isa. 53:1-2). I am not speaking of this natural darkness here. But even these people's minds are prejudiced against the Gospel and darkened to the glory of Christ because of their lusts and desires. (John 1:46, 12:43). This is the difference among people who hear the Word because no one can do anything to receive Jesus and see his glory without the help of God's grace (Matt. 11:25, John 6:44-45).

3. **Tired Christians**. Then there are those of us who are cured and saved from both of these through faith, our eyes of understanding are opened to perceive and discern spiritual things (Eph. 1:16–18). But this cure is only partial while on earth, consisting of many degrees (1 Cor. 13:12). Some have a clearer light than others and discern the mystery of God's wisdom, and of Christ's glory better. But this light is still obstructed and hindered from fully shining, no matter how clearly we see. This is due to the corrupted nature that remains in us, blinding the mind and weakening us spiritually. When we have any corrupt and excessive desires, such as love of the world, worldly thoughts, sensual feelings, or any spiritual disorders, our faith is weakened, especially in discerning and seeing the glory of Christ. The mind becomes unsteady in its search, continually distracted and diverted with useless, selfish thoughts and imaginations.

People suffering from this can have the same doctrinal knowledge of Jesus as we do, and the same evidence of its truth on their minds, but when they try to gain a real understanding of these things, everything becomes dark and confused through the uncertainty and instability of their minds.

Through faith, we have a view of Christ's glory that is weak and unsteady, because of the nature of faith and the way it is revealed to us as a reflection in a mirror. Where our corrupt lusts are indulged and are not continually put to death; where sin dominates the mind, and our faith weakened as a result, we cannot see or meditate on this glory of Christ. This is why many Christians are so weak and unstable when it comes to this, some having no idea of it at all. The light of faith in our minds is impaired, clouded, and darkened by the power of lust; it cannot discover this glory the way it should. This makes preaching Jesus unprofitable for many.

Distracted Minds

When we see Jesus' glory by faith, our minds are filled with thoughts and meditations about him, and our desires are for him. This cannot be separated from a spiritual view of his glory. Everyone that has this view will have many thoughts on and desires for Jesus (Phil. 3:8–10). And if they do not, then maybe they have not heard his voice or seen him, no matter what they say (John 5:37). A spiritual sight of Christ will produce love for him, and if anyone does not love him, they never saw him and do not know him. It is not love if it does not make us think of the beloved. So, anyone who shares in this grace will often think about who Jesus is, what he has done for us, of his love and condescension, of his glorious divine nature used in wisdom and goodness for the salvation of the church. Thoughts and meditations of these things will abound in us if we do not lack faith. Intense desire for him will follow, resulting in a refreshing experience. If these are not there, those people deceive their souls in the hopes of any blessing by Jesus or the Gospel.

Where there are existing sinful problems or excessive desires in the mind—self-love, love of the world, cares and fears about it—they will obstruct and confuse themselves with many thoughts that leave no room for quiet meditations on Christ and his glory. But, where the thoughts are engaged, the desires and emotions, which can stimulate them and be led by them, will also be focused (Col. 3:1-2).

Satan Blinds Us

Our faith is disrupted by the temptations of Satan. His original strategy, wherever the gospel is preached, is to blind people's eyes so the light of the glorious gospel of Christ, who is the image of God, does not shine on them or illuminate their minds (2 Cor. 4:4). He never gives up. No matter how bright the light of the gospel is in preaching the Word, he manages to blind many minds through different schemes, so they see nothing of Jesus' glory. In this way, he continues his rule in the children of disobedience. For those of us who are chosen, God overpowers Satan, shining into our hearts, giving us the knowledge of his glory in the face of Jesus (2 Cor. 4:6). But Satan will never stop. He will try every way to irritate, upset, and blind believers' minds, so they cannot retain clear and distinct views of this glory. He does this in two ways:

1. **Spiritual attacks.** With some people, he uses all his tricks of serpentine subtlety and throws his fiery darts to worry, upset, and discourage them, so they have no easy views of Jesus or his glory. This is where fears, doubts, disputes, and uncertainties come from. Then, they

cannot apprehend the love of Christ, find any interest in it, or know any refreshing persuasions that they are accepted with him. Even if these shine into their minds, they quickly vanish and disappear. Fears that they are rejected by God, that he will not receive them here or in heaven, take their place, and they are filled with anxieties and discouragements, making it impossible to have a clear view of his glory. I know that ignorance, atheism, and stubborn security in sensual sins also add to block all these things. But this is not new, since people claim to be Christians only for their own gain and speak evil of things they do not know about, corrupting themselves in what they know naturally like animals.

2. **False security.** With others, Satan uses other methods. He seduces them into careless security, where they promise peace to themselves without any diligent search into these things. They live in a general presumption that they will be saved by Jesus, although they do not know how. This is why Paul emphasizes self-examination for all Christians: "Examine yourselves, to see whether you are in the faith. Test yourselves. Or do you not realize this about yourselves, that Jesus Christ is in you?—unless indeed you fail to meet the test!" (2 Cor. 13:5). He says we must judge ourselves to see whether Jesus is in us or not. He cannot be in us unless he is received by the faith with which we see his

glory. By faith we receive him, and by faith, he lives in our hearts (John 1:12, Eph. 3:17).

This is the main way the devil continues in the world. Many are seduced, living in the safety of neglecting these things. This false security is an evil destruction of people's souls that is usually only found in those who are unrepentant of huge, public sin. However, to neglect to search for an experience of the power and grace of the gospel in our own hearts is no less destructive than having no repentance for any type of sin.

These and other obstructions to faith are another reason our view of the glory of Christ in this world is weak and unsteady. It temporarily affects their minds and does not fully transform them into his likeness as it is meant to.

Seeing Perfectly

Now, we will look at the view of Jesus' glory we will have in heaven, compared to what we have here on earth. It is stable, always the same, and has no interruption or diversion. This is because of the perfect deliverance from everything that hinders and obstructs it.

Perfect Minds

We can look at the state of our minds in glory. Our souls will be made perfect: "The spirits of the righteous made perfect" (Heb. 12:23) They are free from all the blockages of the flesh, its influence, and the limitation of their powers. They are perfectly purified from instability and unpredictability—all tendencies to everything sensual and carnal, and all methods of self-preservation or ambition—being completely transformed into the image of God in spirituality and holiness. Looking at the state of our bodies after the resurrection, they will be entirely subservient to the most spiritual efforts of our minds in their highest elevation by the light of glory. We will be empowered and built to eternally live in the contemplation of Jesus' glory with joy and satisfaction. Our understanding will always be perfected with the vision of God, and our emotions will be toward it. This is happiness.

Our souls, united with and confined to our bodies, are not able to comprehend and abide constantly in the contemplation of this glory. So, even though our sight of it here is dim and imperfect in the weakness of our minds, we are sometimes forced to turn away from what we understand, as our physical eyes turn from the rays of the sun when it shines brightly. But in this perfect state, they can see and delight in this glory constantly with eternal satisfaction.

"As for me," says David, "I shall behold your face in righteousness; when I awake, I shall be satisfied with your likeness" (Ps. 17:15). It is only Jesus who is the likeness and image of God. When we awake in the other world with our minds purified and rectified, seeing him will always be satisfying to us. There we will never have enough, never get tired, never be reluctant. The mind, being made perfect in all its faculties, powers, and operations, will be satisfied in seeing him forever. And where there is perfect satisfaction, there is happiness forever. So, the Holy Spirit says of the four living creatures, "Day after day and night after night they keep on saying, 'Holy, holy, holy is the Lord God, the Almighty'" (Rev. 4:8). They are continually in admiration and praise of God in Christ without weariness or interruption. This is how we will be like the angels.

Perfect Sight

As our minds will be empowered to comprehend this glory of Jesus, the method of seeing it is much more excellent than faith and absolutely perfect. This is direct vision or sight. On earth, we walk by faith, but there, it is by sight. It is not an external aid, like a telescope helping our weakness to see things at a distance, but it is an internal power, an act of the internal power of our minds where they are endowed in a glorified state. This way we will see him "face to face" (1 Cor. 13:12), as he is, a direct comprehension of his glory. This sight will be given to us for this reason. There, the whole glory of Jesus is clear and evident, giving us eternal acceptance of it.

Eternal Fellowship

Jesus will never again withdraw himself from us or hide the manifestation of himself from our sight. He sometimes does this in this life, and it is necessary for us for him to do it. But there, "we will always be with the Lord" (1 Thess. 4:17) without interruption. This is the center of good and evil when it comes to our future conditions. Eternity makes us absolutely good on the one hand, and absolutely evil on the other. To be in hell is the greatest punishment, to be there forever, without a break from misery. To be in heaven is the life of future happiness.

There are no changes in the heavenly state. The new Jerusalem has no temple in it, "for its temple is the Lord God the Almighty and the Lamb" (Rev. 21:22). There is no need for formal worship or rituals because we will not need more grace or motivation to do these —the constant, immediate, uninterrupted enjoyment of God and the Lamb supplies everything. There is no need for the sun or moon to shine, because the glory of God enlightens it all, and the Lamb is the light. The light of the sun is excellent, but it has seasons, and after it has shone its brightest, it makes way for the night and darkness. The light of the moon is very useful in the night, but it also has its seasons. This is the same as the light we have of the glory of God and the Lamb in this world. Sometimes it is like the light of the sun, which shines seven times brighter in the Gospel than under the Law (Isa. 30:26). Sometimes it is like the light of the moon, bringing relief in the night from temptations and trials. But it is not constant, we are under a variation of light and darkness—we see Christ, and then we lose sight of him. But in heaven, the perpetual presence of Jesus with his saints makes it the noon of light and glory always.

Unlimited Strength

This vision does not become weak because of internal defects or from attacks of temptations, as the sight of faith in this life is. No doubts or fears, no disturbing darts or injections, will be there. No habit, condition, tendency, or attitude will remain in our souls, except what will eternally lead us to contemplate the glory of Christ with joy. There will be no defect in the gracious powers of our souls, and we will have everlasting victory over any opposition (1 Cor. 15:55–57). The mouth of iniquity will be quiet forever, and the voice of Satan will not be heard anymore.

The vision we will have in heaven of the glory of Christ is peaceful—always the same, always new and complete, where nothing can disturb the mind. And when the soul can, without any internal weakness or external hindrances, perform perfectly on the most perfect object, that is where we will have the complete happiness that our nature is capable of.

Whenever we find any contented, refreshing view of Jesus' glory through the revelation in faith, we can do nothing but long after and desire to come to this perfect, abiding, unchanging aspect of it.

Study Guide - Reflections

John Owen takes the concept of faith a step further in this chapter, but he looks at it from a different view. He asks the question we all struggle with at times: "Where are you, Lord?" We might have faith, but we still cannot see or hear him, no matter how hard we pray or fast. It is such a helpful insight into every Christian's walk with Jesus—those moments he feels far or we go through a dry, quiet patch. What do we do in those seasons? Where do we turn?

While he unpacks the reasons and responses, he touches on another very real dilemma in the church today: replacing Jesus with our own image of him. There are still religious establishments that venerate their statues and art to the point of worshiping them. But even in modern churches, Christians find things to hold onto when their faith is tested, things that can be a physical substitute for Jesus so they can see, touch, and "know" him. These are idols, the same as the golden calf the Israelites made in the desert!

1. Have you ever experienced a time when Jesus seemed far, distant, and quiet? What happened?
2. If we have sinned, then it is clear, we need to repent. But why does he sometimes withdraw when we are clear in our hearts and determined in our spirits?
3. Read James 1:2-4. Why does Jesus test our faith?
4. The preaching and reading of the Gospel (not just the first four books of the New Testament, but the glory and grace of Jesus and him crucified) is what bolsters and steadies our faith. Why and how does it do this?
5. Owen speaks of different people and their various responses to the Word of God and to faith. Where do you see yourself in these categories? Do you know others who are far from God, denying his truth and grace? Do you ever pray for them?

14

FINAL THOUGHTS

There are many other differences, but I will only look at two here.

Differences in Perception

In seeing the glory of Christ by faith here on earth, we gradually learn things from the Bible and compare them, so they become the object of what we see—our spiritual comprehension of these things. We do not have it revealed to us in a vision or grand appearance as Isaiah and John had. But we do not need that—it would not be an advantage to us because, through the assurance of our faith, we have a prophecy more useful than a voice from heaven (2 Peter 1:17–19). Those who received such visions, even though they were for the benefit of the church, it was not beneficial for themselves, as one cried out, "Woe is me! For I am lost" and the other "fell at his feet as though dead" (Isa. 6:5, Rev.

1:17). We are not able to bear these glorious representations of him here on earth for our own edification.

Since we do not have external displays of his glory through visions, we also do not have any new revelations of him through immediate inspiration. We see nothing and know nothing except what is shown to us in the Bible. And even in the Bible, there is not one complete proposal of the glory and all that belongs to it because there is no sufficient representation of it on this side of heaven. If all the light of the celestial lights had been contracted into one, it would have been destructive to our eyes, not useful. But God distributed it into the sun, moon, and stars, giving each its own share to declare his glory and to light up the world. So, if the whole revelation of Jesus' glory had been condensed into one text, it would have overwhelmed our minds rather than enlightened us. So, God has distributed the light of it throughout the books of the Old and New Testament, communicating it in parts and degrees for the proper use of the church. In one place, we have a description of his person and its glory. Sometimes these are in plain words, and sometimes in allegories, conveying a spiritual sense to our minds. In others, we read of his love and condescension, and his glory there. His humiliation, exaltation, and power are revealed in different places. And as one star differs from another in glory, so it was that God represented the glory of Christ in types and shadows in the Old Testament, and as it is declared in the New Testament. Descriptive testimonies are planted all through the Bible, which we can collect as flowers in the paradise of God for our faith and sight.

So, the spouse in Song of Songs considered every part of the person and grace of Christ and then concluded that "he is altogether desirable" (Song. 5:10–16). So, we should do the same in our study of the Scripture to find out the revelation of the glory of Jesus there as the prophets did, having received it by immediate inspiration. They "searched and inquired carefully, inquiring what person or time the Spirit of Christ in them was indicating when he predicted the sufferings of Christ and the subsequent glories" (1 Peter 1:10-11). Seeing Jesus bit by bit in revelation is one reason why we see him here only in part.

Some think that by chopping, painting, and decorating, they can make an image of Jesus to perfectly represent him to their senses and emotions. But they feed on ashes and have a lie in their right hand (Isa. 44:20). Jesus Christ is clearly crucified before our eyes in the Bible (Gal. 3:1). So, he is also clearly exalted and glorified there. The wisdom of faith allows us to gather these packaged descriptions of him into one so that they may be the object of our view and contemplation.

In heaven, we will see the whole glory of Christ at once and always before us, and we will be empowered in one act of the light of glory to comprehend it. Here on earth, we are at a loss—our minds and understanding fail us, and our hearts cannot conceive the beauty and glory of this complete representation of Jesus to us. To have the glory of what he is, what he was in his physical state and condition, what he did and suffered, what he is exalted to—his love and condescension, his spiritual union with the church, and the impartation of himself, with the reconciliation of all things in him—and the glory of God the Father, in his wisdom, righteousness, grace, love, goodness, power, shining eternally in him, in what he is, has done, and does—all presented to us in one view, comprehended by us at once, is something we cannot presently conceive. We can long for it, pant after it, and have some samples of it—where our souls will constantly, inseparably, and eternally cling to Jesus in love, in the sight of the glory of his person and grace, until they are watered, dissolved, and soaked in the waters of life and the rivers of pleasure in heaven forever. These are the things we admire, adore, love, long for, have sweet tastes of, and which we cannot fully comprehend.

These are a few of the differences between the view we have here of the glory of Christ, and the one we will have in heaven: faith and sight.

Differences in Effects

Lastly, the difference between them is in their effects.

Transformed

First, the vision we will have of this glory in heaven, and of the glory of God in him, is perfectly and absolutely transforming. It completely changes us into the image of Jesus. When we see him there, we will be as he is; we will be like him because we will see him (1 John 3:2). While the final, perfecting act of this transformation is through seeing his glory, there are many things to take note of, linked to this.

1. The soul, when it leaves the body, is immediately free from all the weakness, darkness, uncertainties, and fears that come from the flesh. The first Adam—the fallen—is then abolished. It is not only freed from all sinful tendencies clinging to our corrupt nature but also from all those sinless grievances and sicknesses that belong to it. Moving from mortality into immortality is a step towards glory. The relief and peace our souls will find in being delivered from this burden is a door to eternal rest. This change is made in the center of all evil—death—as it becomes a method of freeing us from all the remains of what is evil.

Ending our natures brings no advantage with it, especially as it is a part of the curse. But it does through the sanctification of it by the death of Jesus. God's punishment becomes a powerful method for transmitting mercy (1 Cor. 15:22, 54). It is only through Jesus' death that believers' souls are freed by death from sin, infirmity, and evil, which they had from the flesh, the burden under which they groaned. No one knows the extent of this privilege, and the birth of glory in it, who has been worn out through conflicting with the body of death. The soul is freed from all irritations, all marks of the flesh, and is advanced and increased in its gracious abilities.

It is not the same for wicked people. Death is a curse for them and the way of being delivered into evil, not from it. While they were fond of the influences of the flesh, finding joy in them, they will now be deprived of it. Their souls, separated from their bodies, are eternally harassed with all the unsettling passions hammered into their minds by their corrupt fleshly lusts. They look for relief in death, but it is pointless. If there is anything good and useful to them, they will be deprived of it. Their freedom from physical pain cannot match the combination of evil that death will unleash on them.

2. The "spirits of the righteous" are freed by death from the blockage of the flesh—their souls, filled with faith, love, and delight, are immediately free and empowered to focus on God in Christ. The reason they were created, why our nature was given all these godly characteristics, was that we might submit to God in them and come to enjoy him. When they are completely freed from all weakness, wickedness, and disabilities that came through the fall, they are carried toward God, holding onto him with the most intense embraces. Everything they do toward God will be natural with joy, happiness, and peace. We do not know the wonder of how our souls will operate in divine things when they are released from their current burden of the flesh. This is a second step toward the culmination of glory.

In the resurrection of the body, fully redeemed, it will be purified, sanctified, and glorified, without any obstruction to the soul, but will be a holy vessel for its highest and most spiritual function. The body will never be a worry or a burden to the soul anymore, but an assistant and participant in its happiness. Our eyes were made to see our Redeemer, and our other senses to receive notions of him. As the bodies of wicked people are restored to increase and complete their suffering, so the bodies of the righteous will be restored to improve and fulfill their happiness.

3. These things are a preparation for glory. The complete impartation is by the infusion of a new heavenly light into the mind, allowing us to see Jesus as he is. The soul will not be brought into the immediate presence of Christ without being given a new power to be able to see him and the immediate representation of his glory. Faith will stop since it is only necessary on earth while we are absent from Jesus. This light of glory takes its place.
4. In the first work of this light of glory, Christians will see the glory of Christ, and the glory of God in him, and be immediately and completely changed into his likeness. They will be as he is when they see him as he is. There is no growth in glory. The internal light of glory and its transforming power is not capable of degrees, even though new revelations can come to it in eternity. The infinite fountain of life, light, and goodness can never be understood or exhausted. When sin entered, God said, "Behold, the man has become like one of us" (Gen. 3:22), rebuking his design, but when the work of grace was accomplished, he said in love and infinite goodness, "Man is become like one of us," in the perfect restoration of our image

in him. This is the first effect of the light of glory.

In seeing the glory of Christ in this life, faith is accompanied by a transforming power (2 Cor. 3:18). It is the principle and method that all spiritual change happens in us while we are on earth, but it is imperfect in being gradual and partial.

  a. It works gradually and does not immediately transform us into the image of Jesus, and sometimes the degrees of its progress are almost invisible to us. It requires much spiritual wisdom and observation to obtain an experience of this in our own souls. "Our inner self is being renewed day by day," while we see these invisible things (2 Cor. 4:16–18). But how? Just as our physical bodies decay by age, small alterations at a time, so it is with the transformation we have by faith in its present view of the glory of Christ. According to our experience of its power, we find evidence of its truth and reality in seeing him. No one can have the assurance of seeing Jesus and his glory by faith without some effects of it changing them into his likeness. It is like the woman in the Gospel who touched his garment—power went out from him to heal her illness—so our view of faith will trigger a transforming power from Christ to the soul.

     a. It happens partially. It does not complete its work in perfection. The change it brings is great and glorious, it is "one degree of glory to another" (2 Cor. 3:18), a progress of glorious grace, but absolute perfection only happens when we see him with our eyes. Perfection was not by the law. It did many things in preparation to reveal the will of God, but it "made nothing perfect" (Heb. 7:19), so absolute perfection in holiness and the restoration of the image of God is not by the Gospel, is not by faith. However, it prepares us in part (Phil. 3:10–14).

Perfect

Secondly, direct sight is <u>beatifical</u>, meaning it brings perfect rest and happiness to those who have it.

1. There is a continuous work and impartation of God through Jesus in the souls of those who are glorified. All creatures must live in dependence on Him who is the eternal fountain of being, life, and goodness to all, even in heaven. We cannot exist in our beings, lives, souls, bodies, the inner and outer man, without the continual work of divine power in us, and toward us. So, in the glorified state, everything depends eternally on divine power and goodness, transmitting themselves to us, for all we need to live in heaven.
2. We cannot understand the way these are imparted to us. We cannot even understand the nature and way of his spiritual Impartation to us in this life. We know these things by their signs and by the effects they produce in the real

change of our natures, but we see little of them. "The wind bloweth where it listeth, and we hear the sound thereof, but we know not whence it cometh, and whither it goeth; so is every one that is born of the Spirit" (John 3:8). All God's real works in heaven and earth are incomprehensible, acts of infinite power that we cannot search to perfection.

3. All transmissions from God and fullness in heaven to glorified saints are in and through Jesus, who will always be the medium of communication between God and the church, even in glory. Everything will be gathered into one head in him, in heaven and earth—dependent on God—this order will never be dissolved (Eph. 1:10-11, 1 Cor. 3:23). These communications from God through Jesus carry our existence of happiness and glory. We will not be more self-sufficient in glory than we are in grace on the earth.

4. The way we will receive these transmissions from God by Jesus—eternal springs of life, peace, joy, and happiness—is this direct sight. The Bible says very clearly that it contains the perfect operation of our minds and souls in a perfect state, on the most perfect object, and is the only way to holiness and happiness. This is why there can never be any over-indulgence or exhaustion in heaven when we see this glory. Not only is the object we look at absolutely infinite, without an end or a depth, but our happiness which consists of continuous fresh impartations from the infinite fullness of his

nature, is always new, and always will be so throughout eternity. All the saints of God will drink from the rivers of pleasure at his right hand, be satisfied with his likeness, and refresh themselves in the eternal springs of life, light, and joy forever.

Final Thoughts

The view we have by faith of Jesus' glory in this world does not produce this effect. It is sanctifying, not glorifying. The best Christians are far from a perfect or glorified state in this life, not just because of the external evil they are exposed to, but also of the weakness and imperfection of their inner being in grace. But we can see some things that honor the faith in those who have received it.

1. Focusing on Jesus will allow Christian souls to participate in future glory beforehand, forming their attitudes and preparing them to enjoy it.
2. There is no glory, peace, joy, or satisfaction in this world that compares with what we receive by that weak and imperfect view of the glory of Jesus by faith. All the joys of the world are nothing in comparison to what we receive.
3. It is enough to give us a foretaste of future happiness in the enjoyment of Jesus, to continually motivate us to long after and pant for it. But it is not beatifical.

There are other differences between our seeing the glory of Jesus in this life by faith and that direct vision of it in heaven, but I will not look at those. There is nothing more for us to do than fill our meditations on it with the deepest humility, out of a sense of our unworthiness and insufficiency to comprehend those things, admiration of that excellent glory which we cannot comprehend, and passionate desires for that time when we will see him as he is, always be with him, and know him even as we are known.

Study Guide - Reflections

The difference between faith and direct heavenly sight continues in this chapter. Owen focuses on the difference between our abilities to see as humans and our enhanced capabilities as renewed spiritual beings. He goes into depth with this subject to ensure we do not get lost as it can be a topic that totally escapes our logic or seems too airy-fairy to be true. But as Christians, the Bible is full of verses speaking of this change that will one day happen.

Owen also looks at this change, how our transformation into Jesus' image here on earth is gradual, sometimes painful, often demanding faith and perseverance. We are being made into his likeness, a process that continues to the day we are suddenly face-to-face with him. While we long to be free of this body so we can be with him, we must still endure all the obstacles, temptations, and weaknesses that face us every day on earth.

1. Read Ephesians 1:13-14.
2. Do you long to be with Jesus or are you one of those who have many lists and things to get

done and experience before going to heaven? Why do you think we sometimes have these tendencies?
3. What excites you most about leaving this earthly body behind?
4. Why do you think it is necessary for Jesus to work so gradually, bit by bit, day by day, instead of quickly and suddenly?
5. What are the three things we can see in those Christians who are sanctified by seeing Jesus' glory and honored for their faith?
6. Do you possess any of these in your own spiritual life?

15

PERSUASION FOR UNBELIEVERS

Here, we need to look at some issues when the truth is declared to those who need it. There are two headings we can use to look at these.

The first is directed at those who are still strangers to this holy and glorious One, not yet participants of him, or have any real interest in him. And the second will be directed to Christians as a guide and assistance for their recovery from spiritually backsliding, and reviving the spring of grace, holiness, and obedience in them.

Wherever there is a declaration of Jesus and his attributes, person, grace, or role, it should be accompanied by an invitation and encouragement for sinners to come to him. Jesus used this method and told us to do the same (Matt. 11:27–30, John 7:37-38). It is necessary to bring people to consider Jesus' glory, to engage and invite lost sinners to this.

An Invitation to the Lost

Think About Your State

Let them think about their present state with respect to God and eternity. This Moses wanted for the Israelites: "If they were wise, they would understand this; they would discern their latter end!" (Deut. 32:29). It is the greatest mistake to leave these issues in uncertainty; and that man who cannot prevail with himself strictly to examine what is his state and condition with respect unto eternity does never do any good nor abstain from any evil in a due manner. Remember that "many are called, but few are chosen." To be called is to enjoy all blessings of the Gospel—which is all you unto whom I speak can pretend unto; yet this you may do and not be chosen—even to those whom the word is preached, there are only a few that will be saved.

When Jesus grouped the hearers of the word into four different types of ground, it was only one that benefitted. If our congregations are no better than the people listening to him, there is only a quarter that will be saved, maybe less, and is it not strange that every one of them is not jealous of himself and his own condition? Many deceive themselves until they are unpleasantly surprised. This is shown in the final judgment, where most who professed the Gospel are complaining about their disappointments at the end of their lives (Matt. 25:41–44).

Be Careful of Presuming

Do not be deceived by common presumptions. Most people have some idea about what state they are in, and what needs attention, but they do not diligently look into it because a number of common presumptions jump into their minds. They think they are different and better than others, and as Christians, they have light and convictions, so they abstain from sin and perform duties that others do not. Everyone else, they judge to be in a worse condition. Do not trust or rely on such people who have no desire to come to Jesus and identify with him. This was part of John the Baptist's message: "Do not presume to say to yourselves, 'We have Abraham as our father'" (Matt. 3:9). Their only privilege was in the temple and covenant advantages, but they rested and trusted in these to their ruin, and John wanted to enlighten them.

Think About Eternal Danger

What does it mean to live and die without any interest in Jesus, without him in your life? If this is not on your mind, where thoughts of it are not continuous, there can be no steps taken toward him. Unless we are thoroughly convinced that without him, we are backsliding from God, under the curse, fit for eternal judgment, as some of the worst of God's enemies, we will never run to him for refuge. "Those who are well have no need of a physician, but those who are sick." Jesus "came not to call the righteous, but sinners;" and the conviction intended is the main reason for the law (Mark 2:17). We can tell people about it a thousand times, but they take no notice, do not believe, or see the need to have it preached, because they are not concerned about it. But preachers must say these things so whoever thinks on them might believe them. It is not common for people to ask, "Am I like that?" If we tell these people again that not being interested in Jesus, not being grafted into him by faith, means they run in vain, that all their work in Christianity is lost, that their duties are all rejected, that they are under the anger and curse of God, that their end is eternal destruction, they will ignore them without another thought.

Unless there is a full conviction of the terrible, desperate condition of every soul, no matter what quality, profession, religion, or status, who is not yet part of Jesus, everything else I say has no significance. But the reflection of your state is your main concern in this world, so do not be afraid to take in a full and deep awareness of it, because if you are delivered from it, and it is evident, then you can give eternal praise and thanksgiving. If not, it is extremely necessary that your thoughts are focused on it. This conviction is the first sign of true Christianity. Most religions in the world pretend to have this and so people do not think it is necessary and are never convinced of how lost they are.

See Jesus' Love

Let us look at the condescension and love of Jesus as he invites and calls you to come to him for life, deliverance, mercy, grace, peace, and eternal salvation. There are many of these invitations in the Bible, and they all have encouragements that God knows are suitable for lost, convinced sinners in their state and condition. It is good to study these and see the mixture of wisdom and persuasive grace in them, the force and power of the imploring and argument that goes with them, as found in the Bible.

Jesus speaks to us like this:

Why will you die? Why will you perish? Why will you not have compassion on your own souls? Can your hearts endure, or can your hands be strong, in the day of judgment that is coming? It is not long before all your hopes, reliefs, and presumptions will forsake you, and leave you eternally miserable. Look to me and be saved. Come to me, and I will remove your sins, sorrows, fears, burdens, and give rest to your souls. Come, I beg you, lay aside all procrastinations, all delays, and do not put me off anymore. Eternity is at the door. Cast out all cursed, self-deceiving reservations. Do not hate me and perish rather than accept deliverance by me.

Jesus proclaims, pleads, and urges many things like these on the souls of sinners (Prov. 1:20–33). He does it by preaching the word as if he is with you, standing with you, and speaking personally to each of you. Because it does not suit his present state of glory, he has appointed the ministers of the gospel to stand before you, declaring his invitations in his name (2 Cor. 5:19-20).

- Why is his condescension, grace, and love for you?
- Does God need you?
- Do you deserve this from him?
- Did you love him first?
- Can he be happy without you?
- Does he have a reason and plan for calling you to himself?

Nothing but overflowing mercy, compassion, and grace makes us do it. This is where many souls fall into death and condemnation far more severe than those under the curse of the law (2 Cor. 2:15-16). In their hatred for Jesus' coming to earth in his invitation of sinners to himself lies the sting and poison of unbelief, which inevitably leads to the eternal ruin of their souls. And who will be merciful to those who are guilty of this in eternity?

Know You Will Be Received

When we receive this invitation and begin to look and come to him, we can become afraid that when it comes to judgment, he will not receive us because no heart can conceive, no tongue can express, what terrible, evil sinners we have been. As we are, we have no hope of being accepted by him. Some people come so far as to be aware of the struggles, what difficulties lie in their way, and what objections they have, but they die in their foolishness because they will not consider their state, what is required of them, or how it will be in the end. But when they blame not being accepted by Jesus on their own unworthiness, and are discouraged from coming to him because of it, then there are arguments to convict and persuade them that only the devil and unbelief can defeat.

Instead, we see here that Jesus is ready to receive every sinner that will come to him, which is evidence of God's wisdom and grace for us. This is the language of the Gospel, of everything Jesus did or suffered. It is the testimony of the "three that bear witness in heaven: the Father, the Word, and the Holy Spirit" and of the "three that bear witness on earth: the Spirit, the water, and the blood" (1 John 5:7-8 NKJV). These all testify that Jesus is ready to receive all sinners that come to him.

Those who do not accept God as Father, Son, and Spirit, call him a liar. Whatever Jesus is in his person—representing the Father—what he did on the earth, and what he does in heaven, proclaims the same truth. Nothing but stubborn sin and unbelief can make us think he is not willing to receive us when we come to him. We must speak against the unbelief of all to whom the gospel is preached that do not come to him. Unbelief is contempt for the wisdom of God, a denial of his truth or faithfulness, an impeachment of the sincerity of Jesus in his invites, making him a deceiver. This results in specific hatred for his person and role, and of the wisdom of God in him.

Believe He Can Save You

He is as able to save us because he is ready and willing to receive us. The testimonies that he has given us about his goodness and love are overwhelming; no one can question or deny his power. Generally, it is taken for granted that Jesus is able to save us if he wants to, even though we live in sin and unbelief. And many expect that he will do so because they believe he can if he will. But Jesus has no such power, no such ability—he cannot save unbelieving, unrepentant sinners. This cannot be done without denying himself, acting against his word, and destroying his own glory. No one should believe this fantasy. Jesus is able to save those, and only those, who come to God through him. While you live in sin and unbelief, Jesus cannot save you. But when it comes to judgment day, some think that even though they do not believe Jesus cannot save them, they think they cannot be saved by him. His power to save those who obey his call is sovereign, uncontainable, and almighty—nothing can stand in its way. Everything in heaven and earth is committed to him—all power is his—and he will use it to save everyone that comes to him.

Think About His Glory

When we think about the representation of God and his holy character, it should encourage us to come to him, because we have seen he is wise and glorious, and has used all his mercy, love, grace, goodness, righteousness, wisdom, and power to save those who believe. Whoever comes to Jesus by faith on this representation of the glory of God in him, gives God all the glory and honor which he desires from us. We can do nothing else that pleases him more. Every poor soul that comes in faith to Jesus gives God all the glory. What more can we do? There is more glory given to God by coming to Christ in believing, than in keeping the whole law. He has revealed the holy attributes of his nature more through salvation by Christ than in giving the law. There is no one who believes but refuses to come to Jesus because secretly, through sin and unbelief, they hate God and all his ways, and do not want his glory exalted or manifested, choosing rather to die in hostility than to give glory to him. Do not deceive yourselves or be apathetic about whether or not you will come to Jesus or not, as if it is something you can put off until another time. Your refusal now is one of the biggest acts of hostility against God that you are capable of.

The Glory of Christ | 205

Think About Your Eternal Future

When we come to Jesus, we have an interest in this glory. Jesus will become ours more intimately than our wives and children, and so all his glory is ours too. We are all affected by the good things in our relationships —grace, riches, beauty, and power—we have an interest in them, because of our relationship with them. Jesus is nearer to believers than any natural relationships, giving them an interest in his glory. Is this a small thing in your eyes, that Jesus will be yours, and all his glory will be yours, and you will benefit from it eternally? Do you still want to be a stranger to all this glory? Do you want to be left with your share of this world in lusts, sins, and temporary pleasures with eternal ruin at the end, while such an indestructible substance and riches of glory are offered to you?

The Ungratefulness of Refusing Him

Lastly, consider the horrible ingratitude there is when we refuse to come to Jesus when he invites us. "How shall we escape, if we neglect so great salvation?" Impenitent unbelievers who hear the gospel are the worst and most ungrateful of God's creation. Even the demons who are wicked, are not guilty of this sin, because Jesus is never offered to them—they never had an opportunity for salvation on faith and repentance. This is their sin and will be their misery for eternity. "Hear, ye despisers, wonder, and perish." The sin of the devil is in hatred and opposition to knowledge, above what the nature of man is in this world. Men, therefore, must sin in some instance above the devil, For God to sentence people to the same eternal end as the devil and his angels, means they have a sin greater than the devil's—this is unbelief.

The Urgency of His Invitation

- What must we do?
- What shall we dedicate ourselves to?
- What is required of us?

1. Take the advice of the Bible:

Today, if you hear his voice, do not harden your hearts as in the rebellion, on the day of testing in the wilderness... But exhort one another every day, as long as it is called "today," that none of you may be hardened by the deceitfulness of sin. (Heb. 3:7-13).

This day is the grace of acceptable time—the day of salvation. Others have also had this day and missed their opportunity—watch out in case it is the same with you. Now if someone writes it down or remembers it, it might read like this: "Today there was an invitation of Jesus and salvation in him given to my heart. From this time, I decide to give up myself to him." If you decide, accept the responsibility of what you are doing, and realize that if you turn away, it is a sign that you are in danger.

2. Know that it is time for you to decide about Christianity; do not remain in suspense, always question of whether you want to be saved or not. This is as good a time and season as any for a decision while you are on earth. Many

things can happen between this and the next opportunity that will put you off track and make entering the kingdom of heaven far more difficult than before. It will also make living in this world uncertain because now knowing what will become of you in eternity is a miserable kind of life. Those who ignore judgment day and live after lusts and pleasures have a present satisfaction and do not say, "It is hopeless," because they "found new life for… strength" (Isa. 57:10), but you have nothing to refresh you, neither will your end be better than theirs if you die without any interest in Jesus. So, come to a clear decision about what you will do. Jesus has waited a long time for you, and who knows how soon he may withdraw, never to look for you again.

Objections to His Invitation

It is also necessary to remove some of those common and obvious excuses that sinners usually make to put off coming to Jesus. Even though it is unbelief, acting in the darkness of people's minds and their stubborn wills, that keeps sinners from answering his call, it disguises itself so it is not so blatant and ugly.

There is no sin that people can be guilty of that is so horrible and dreadful as unbelief, when exposed in spiritual light. With Satan's help, it suggests other claims and deceptions to sinners' minds that they used to refuse to come to Christ. (2 Cor. 4:4). It can be anything, but not unbelief—that they reject. So, I will look at a few of those excuses and evasions which are shown in the Bible.

What More Can You Do?

First, there are people who will ask: What do you want us to do? We hear the word preached, we believe it as much as we can, we do many things willingly and abstain from evil. What else is required of us?

1. It is normal for those who do follow the ways of God, but not in everything, and so nothing that requires more from them than what they already do. So, the people dispute with God himself (Mal. 1:6, 3:8-13). Those in the Gospel who thought they had done their duty, being convinced of faith in Jesus, asked him with indignation, "What must we do, to be doing the works of God?" (John 6:28). If what we are doing is not enough, what more do you require of us? It was the same with the young man who asked, "What do I still lack?" (Matt. 19:20). Do not be too confident of your state, in case you lack that one thing which will lead to your eternal ruin.
2. There are many people like this where there is not one spark of saving faith in them. Simon the magician heard the word and believed as best he could; Herod heard it and did many things with gladness; and many hypocrites do many things when convicted, abstaining from many sins: but no more when it comes to his invitation, so they perish forever.

3. Some are sincere but are without faith, it is not in them. There is a fundamental act of faith, where we meet with Christ and receive him. It must come before all other duties and occasions —it is laying the foundation, and other things build on it. This, you must take hold of. You will know this faith by these two things:
   a. **It is unique.** So, our Savior tells the Jews, "This is the work of God, that you believe in him whom he has sent" (John 6:29). The act, work, or duty of faith, in the receiving of Christ, is a strange, singular work, where the soul surrenders in obedience to God. It is not the same as those common duties mentioned, but the soul exclusively joins with Jesus on God's command.
   b. **It is spiritual.** There is a spiritual change that happens in the soul. "If anyone is in Christ, he is a new creation. The old has passed away; behold, the new has come" (2 Cor. 5:17). If you do not choose to deceive and ruin your soul, examine whether you have received Jesus Christ in this extraordinary, transforming act of faith: Do not deceive yourself out of obeying with this advice.

Why Should I Keep Trying?

Some will say they do not know how to continue in this work. They do not understand it. They have tried to believe, but still fail in what they intend to do. They go on and off but make no progress, finding no satisfaction. So, they think it best to stop without troubling themselves anymore in the act of faith in receiving Jesus. This is the language of people's hearts, but not their mouths: another shelter of unbelief. They act accordingly but have a secret sadness that keeps them from attempting a real meeting with Jesus. There are a few things that can be said for these people.

Persevere

Remember the disciples that were fishing and had tried all night but caught nothing (Luke 5:3-4). When Jesus came to them, he told them to throw out their nets once more. Peter makes some excuse about working through the night in vain, however, he tried once more on the command of Jesus and had an astonishing catch of fish. Have you been exhausted with disappointments in your attempts? Throw in your net once more on Jesus' command—try once again to come to him on his call and invitation. You do not know what success he may give to you.

Keep Persisting

Realize that it is not failing in your attempts to come to Jesus, but giving up in your efforts, that will be your ruin. The woman of Canaan, when she cried to Jesus for mercy was rejected and resisted (Matt. 15:22-28). First, he did not answer her. Then his disciples wanted him to send her away, so she would not trouble him anymore. At this, he gave a reason why he would not regard her, or why he could ignore her—she was not an Israelite. But she does not give up, pressing into his presence and crying out for mercy. Having reached a point where her faith was tested to its limit, which was his plan from the beginning, he says she is like a dog that should not have children's bread given to it. If she had given up because of this severe rebuke, she would never have gained mercy, but persisting in her request, she at last succeeded.

You may have prayed, cried, and promised without success. Sin has broken through all. However, if you do not give up, you will succeed in the end. You do not know what time God will come in with his grace, and Jesus will manifest his love to you as he did with the poor woman, after many rebukes. He might do it today, and if not, he might do it another—do not despair. Take Jesus' words as encouragement, "Blessed is the one who listens to me, watching daily at my gates, waiting beside my doors" (Prov. 8:34). If you hear him and wait, even though you have entered, standing at the gates and door, yet in this, you will be blessed.

Don't Discourage

The rule in this is, "Let us know; let us press on to know" (Hos. 6:3). Do you want to know Jesus, hear the word, and continue in sincere efforts in holy duties? Even though you cannot find any evidence that you have received him or have met with him, nothing can destroy you except giving up. Then you will know if you continue on to know the Lord. Many people can tell you their experiences, that if they had been discouraged by present overwhelming difficulties, arising from their disappointments, breaking of promises, and relapses into foolishness, they would have been completely ruined. But now they are at rest and peace in Jesus' embrace. Jesus lost many disciples in one moment, and they lost their souls. They "turned back and no longer walked with him" (John 6:66). Pay attention to these things.

Putting It Off

Some people may say that they do the things that are necessary, knowing they must come to Jesus by believing, or they will be lost. But this is not the time—there will be enough time later to do this when everything else has finished. Now, they do not have time to enter in and do this. They stay in their present state for a while, hearing and doing many things, and when they have the time, do what is necessary.

Foolishness of Waiting

This is evidence of the lazy, foolish nature of sin—a deprivation that the apostle says is one of the main evils of corrupted nature (Tit. 3:1–3). Can anything be more foolish and stupid than for people to put off thinking about the eternal state of their souls for one hour, especially when they have no idea if they will be alive in the next hour or not? They prefer present trivialities and misery of an immortal state rather than eternal happiness. For those who have never heard of these things, who never had any conviction of sin and judgment, this is not the place you want to be in. But for you who have Jesus preached to you, who knows the necessity of coming to him, to put it off from day to day because of small thoughts—it is a shocking madness! Have you not been spoken to in the language of the Wisdom of God? (Prov. 6:9–11). You come to hear the word, and when you go away, the language of your hearts is, "A little sleep, a little slumber, a little folding of the hands to rest" (Prov. 24:33); we will stay as we are for now, and later wake up. Many perish every day because of this deceit. This is a dark shadow that hides cursed unbelief.

Satan's Strategy

This is the main strategy Satan uses in the world to ruin people's souls who have heard the word preached. He has other schemes, ways, and methods of dealing with other people through sensual and worldly lusts, but for those who are convicted and hear God's Word preached, this is his best technique. He convinces them that there is no rush in this matter—another time will be better—you cannot fail before you die. Today, right now, is not the right moment: you have other things to do; you cannot leave your present state; you can come again to hear the word next time. Realize that if you are influenced to delay coming to Jesus in such a way, you are under the power of Satan, and he is likely to hold you tight until destruction.

Delays Always Come

This is an evil and dangerous attitude to have. If you have learned to put off God and Jesus and the word for the time being, and tell yourself that you do not intend to reject them forever but will respond to them later, you are hardened against all convictions and persuasions. There is only one answer you have: you will do everything required of you some time. This is how many souls are destroyed every day. It is better dealing with men who openly reject than with those who offer meaningless promises (Isa. 5:7-10).

Your Last Chance?

Remember that the Bible specifies today, without any indication that you will have another day or another offer of grace and mercy later (2 Cor. 6:2, Heb. 3:7-13, 12:15). Watch out in case you fall short of God's grace and miss out by missing your opportunity. Redeem the time, or you are lost forever.

Separating Jesus From Everyday Life

As for all your circumstances and responsibilities, there is a way to disappoint the deceit of Satan: mix thoughts of Jesus and the renewal of your decision to come to him with all your daily routines and chores. Do not let anything put it completely out of your mind. Make it familiar to you, and you will beat Satan out of that stronghold (Prov. 7:4). However, shake yourselves out of this dust, or destruction lies at the door.

Too Big a Sacrifice

Some have the language within their hearts that if they surrender and become serious about this duty, they must give up and renounce all their lusts and pleasures. Many of the things and associations where they find so much satisfaction, they do not know how to let go of. If they hold onto their old ways, at least some of them, it would be different, but this total surrender of everything is very severe.

The Jesuits, when they preached Jesus among some of the locals, hid his cross and sufferings from them, telling them only of his glory and power. So, they pretended to win them over to faith in him, hiding things that would discourage them—they preached a false Jesus, one they had designed. We must never do anything like this. We cannot have any arrogance, agreement, or compromise with any sin or lust. We have no right to answer Lot's request: "is it not a little one?—and my life will be saved!" (Gen. 19:20). We cannot agree with Naaman's terms, "In this matter may the LORD pardon your servant" (2 Kings 5:18).

We must be direct and straightforward, no matter the circumstance. If you are discouraged by it, we cannot help that. Anyone who encourages you to come to Christ with hopes of still indulging in any sin is to be cursed. I do not say this as though you could absolutely and perfectly leave all sin immediately, in its roots and branches, but you are to do it in heart and decision, putting all sin to death by the grace from above that helps you. However, your choice must be absolute, without reservation: God or the world, Jesus or Satan, holiness or sin. There is no middle, no compromise (2 Cor. 6:15–18).

Whatever you think about your pleasures, the truth is you have never had any real pleasure yet, nor do you know what it is. If only it was that easy to declare the foolishness, vanity, bitterness, and poison of those things which you have esteemed your pleasures! Only in Jesus are true pleasures and long-lasting riches to be found—these are like pleasant streams, flowing into the ocean of eternal pleasures above. A few moments in these joys are to be preferred above the cursed pleasures of this world (Prov. 3:13–18).

Not That Bad

Some say that they do not see Christians to be any better than they are, so there is no need to urge us so seriously to choose this change. We do not know why we should not be described as believers already like them. Let us put this stumbling block out of the way, even though it is a heavy one.

1. Among those who claim to be believers, there are many false, corrupt hypocrites, and it is no surprise that they become a stumbling block in their iniquities before others. But they will face their own burden and judgment.
2. Some look like true believers, but their pride, covetousness, or carelessness is exposed in their conversation, the way they dress, and their conformity to the world. We confess that God is displeased with them, Jesus and the Gospel are dishonored in this way, many weak are wounded, and others discouraged. But as for you, this is not your way—only so that you will never fall into it.
3. The world does not know, nor is able to judge believers; neither do you, because it is the spiritual person alone that discerns the things of God. Their weaknesses are visible to all, but their graces are invisible—the King's daughter is glorious within. And when you are able to make a correct judgment of them, you will desire nothing more than to be one of them (Ps. 16:3).

These few examples of how unbelief covers its deformity and hides the destruction in it are enough for this purpose. These are multiplied in people's minds, impregnated by the suggestions of Satan on their darkness and foolishness. A little spiritual wisdom will tear open the veil of them all and expose the unbelief acting against Jesus.

Study Guide - Reflections

If you are reading this book and you realize that perhaps you are far off the mark and maybe your spiritual life is more like those who don't have Jesus than those who are born again Christians, then you are in the right place. Jesus never wants anyone to be left behind, denied an opportunity, or passed over. He extends his mercy and grace to everyone, even you. It's time to speak to God, to be real and open about where you are. And then, it's important to let someone in church know about this wonderful step you're taking so they can help you along the proper way, not a superficial path.

Maybe you have already been born again, and you're sure of it. There's still a part for you to play as we read in this chapter. We need to preach on all occasions, bringing the gospel to those in the hope that they have soft, ready soil in their hearts. We need to pray that Jesus will reach them so they too can see and experience God's glory.

1. Why is it important to realize exactly what Jesus has done for each of us as sinners? Why

should we always remember and never forget? Read Psalm 51:12.
2. Why do you think people often put off responding to God's invitation?
3. What does Owen mean when he says, "It is not failing in your attempts of coming to Jesus but giving up in your efforts, that will be your ruin"?
4. What is Satan's main strategy in ruining people's souls who hear the word preached to them?
5. Why do some churches avoid preaching or talking about suffering? Why is it important to acknowledge and embrace this part of Christianity? Read Philippians 1:29.
6. Why is unbelief such a problem, not just with unbelievers but also with Christians? Read Mark 9:23-24.

16

DIRECTION FOR BELIEVERS

This second part is for believers, especially those who have already been walking in the ways of God and the gospel. I want to show that a steady, spiritual view of Jesus' glory by faith will give them a revival from inner decay and fresh springs of grace when they get older. This is confirmed in the Bible through the examples and experiences of many believers and is important for all Christians.

There are two things that Christians who have been in the gospel for many years desire when they are getting close to being in heaven. The one is, that all their cracks will be repaired, their decays recovered, and their backslidings healed, because these they have hated while walking before God. The other is that they may have fresh springs of spiritual life and energetic work of divine character in being spiritually minded, holy, and fruitful, to be able to praise God, honor the gospel, and increase their own peace and joy. These things they value more than anything in the world; they think about these things night and day. For those who do not, whatever they pretend, they are in the dark about themselves and their condition because it is the nature of grace to grow and increase this way. When rivers get closer to the ocean, the more water they have, the faster the flow becomes, so grace will flow more freely and fully as it approaches the ocean of glory.

The experience of grace thriving in us toward the end of our lives is what supports us through the troubles and temptations of life, which we struggle with. Paul tells us that this is our great relief in all our distresses and afflictions, "so we do not lose heart. Though our outer self is wasting away, our inner self is being renewed day by day" (2 Cor. 4:16). During the daily decays of the physical body, as it slowly dies, if we have inner spiritual revivals and renovation, we will not faint in what we face. Without these continual renovations, we will not stand in our troubles, whatever else we have, or whatever we pretend to the contrary.

It is God's holy and wise provision that afflictions and troubles increase with age. It is the same for ministers of the gospel who share in Peter's lot, which Jesus declared to him:

When you were young, you used to dress yourself and walk wherever you wanted, but when you are old, you will stretch out your hands, and another will dress you and carry you where you do not want to go. (John 21:18)

The natural illnesses and weaknesses that come with the decay and troubles of life usually grow worse until all we want is to say the words of Job: "I shall die in my nest" (Job 29:18). So was it with Jacob: after all his hard work to provide for his family, his old age seemed to bring things that almost broke his heart. Often, both persecutions and public dangers come upon them at the same time. While the physical body is perishing, we need lots of support so that we do not faint. This is only found in an experience of daily spiritual renovations in the inner person.

We see this mercy in these verses:

The righteous flourish like the palm tree and grow like a cedar in Lebanon. They are planted in the house of the Lord; they flourish in the courts of our God. They still bear fruit in old age; they are ever full of sap and green, to declare that the Lord is upright; he is my rock, and there is no unrighteousness in him. (Ps. 92:12–15)

The promise in the 12th verse is about the Messiah, or of the New Testament because it is prophesied that "in his days may the righteous flourish" (Ps. 72:7) through the abundance of grace that comes from his fullness (John 1:16, Col. 1:19). In this, we have the glory of the gospel, and not in physical prosperity or external rituals of worship. The prosperity of the righteous in grace and holiness is the glory of Jesus' work and of the gospel. Without this, there is no glory in Christianity. The glory of kings is in the wealth and peace of their subjects, and the glory of Jesus is in the grace and holiness of his subjects.

This prosperity and flourishing are compared to the palm and cedar trees. The palm is beautiful and fruitful, and the cedar is one of the largest and longest-growing trees. So, the righteous are compared to the palm because of the beauty of their declaration and fruitfulness in obedience and to the cedar for their continual, constant growth and increase in grace. It is like this with everyone that is righteous, unless they fall into sinful neglect, as many do these days. Those people are more like a "shrub in the desert, and shall not see any good come" (Jer 17:6). They obscure the glory of Jesus and his kingdom and disturb their own souls.

The words in verse 13, "They are planted in the house of the Lord; they flourish in the courts of our God," do not differentiate as if only some of the nourishing righteous were planted this way, but it describes them all, adding how they are able to grow and flourish. It is being planted in the house of the Lord—in the church, the center of all spiritual life for growth and flourishing —which God is pleased to give believers. To be planted in the house of the Lord is to be fixed and rooted in the grace transmitted by worship. Unless we are planted in the house of the Lord, we cannot flourish in his courts (Ps. 1:3). Unless we are part of the grace of the church, we cannot flourish in a fruitful Christianity. Physical participation is common for hypocrites, who bear some leaves but never grow like the cedar or bear fruit like the palm. So, Paul prays for believers, that Jesus may live in their hearts by faith, that they may be "rooted and grounded in love" and "rooted and built up in him and established" (Eph. 3:17, Col. 2:7). Not having this is the reason we have so many fruitless Christians—they have entered the courts of God by calling themselves believers but were never planted in his house by faith and love. Let us not deceive ourselves—we may be in the church and share in its physical privileges, but not be planted in it so we flourish in grace and fruitfulness.

What I want to point out here is the grace and privilege in verse 14, "They still bear fruit in old age; they are ever full of sap and green." There be three things found in a spiritual state that belongs to the life of God.

1. That Christians will be fat by the heavenly juice, sap, or fatness of the true olive—Jesus (Rom. 11:17). This is the principle of spiritual life and grace that comes from him. When this abounds in them, giving them strength and energy in exercising grace, to keep them from decay and withering away, they are said to be fat—a biblical phrase for being strong and healthy.
2. That they flourish in the abundance and lushness of Christianity because lively grace will produce a flourishing Christianity.
3. That they still bear fruit in all their holy practice.

All these are promised to them, even in old age.

Even trees when they grow old will lose their juice and freshness, and people in old age are subject to all sorts of degeneration, both outward and inward. It is rare to see an elderly person naturally energetic, healthy, and strong. It is also rare to see people spiritually like this at the same season! But this is promised to believers as a special grace and privilege, beyond the growth or fruit-bearing of plants and trees.

The intended grace is for when believers are under all sorts of physical and natural decay, and are also overcome with spiritual decay, then there is provision in the covenant to make them fat, flourishing, and fruitful—vigorous in the power of inner grace and flourishing in their obedience of Christian duties.

Blessed be God for this encouraging word of his grace against all the decays and temptations of old age which we have to struggle with!

Verse 15 of the Psalm reveals the greatness of this privilege: *"To declare that the Lord is upright; he is my rock, and there is no unrighteousness in him."* Look at the oppositions that come against believers being able to flourish in old age: the difficulties and temptations that must be conquered, the actions of the mind above its natural abilities which are not as young and sharp, the tiredness that occurs in a long spiritual conflict, the cries of the flesh to be spared—Nothing else could produce this mighty effect. So, the prophet, dealing with the same promise, ends his discussion with this wonderful remark: "Whoever is wise, let him understand these things; whoever is discerning, let him know them; for the ways of the Lord are right, and the upright walk in them" (Hos. 14:9). Spiritual wisdom will make us see that the faithfulness and power of God work to preserve believers so they can flourish and be fruitful to the end.

Having laid the foundation of this testimony, I will go further to show the application of this—the way we are made participants of this grace is by a steady view of the glory of Christ, as proposed to us in the Gospel.

There is a final spring in the year, a spring in autumn that is faint and weak, but something the gardener cannot do without. The barren ground is evidence of it not coming toward the end of the year. God, the good gardener, looks for the same from us, especially if we had a summer's drought in spiritual decays (Ps. 32:4). With no latter spring the year before, the land suffers during the summer drought. If we have a spiritual drought as God, the good gardener, looks for a latter spring in us in the vigorous work of grace and fruitful obedience, so without it, we cannot have peace or joy in own souls. If a person has made a great appearance of Christianity in their younger days, and then becomes dead, cold, worldly, and selfish when they are older, they have no fresh springs of spiritual life; this is evidence of a barren heart that was never fruitful to God. I know that many need this warning to think diligently about their state and condition.

It is true that the latter spring rain does not bring the same fruit as the one before. There is nothing else needed except for the ground to be good and do what it must in that season. Certain people may have been active and vibrant when they were just born again, but then they are carried in a stream of warm, natural emotions, and might not be so abundant in the latter spring of old age. But those which are proper for the season—spirituality, heavenly-mindedness, separation from the world, ready for the cross and death—are necessary to show we have a living principle of grace, and that God is righteous. He is our rock, and there is no unrighteousness in him.

There are four more things to look at here:

Constant Spiritual Growth

The spiritual life is made to thrive, grow, and increase to the end, and will do so, unless those who have it do not engage in it.

It is different from temporary faith which flourishes for a season and bears some fruit, but there is no nature and design to abide, grow, and increase, only to decay and wither (Matt. 13:20-21). Either some temptation extinguishes it, or it decays until the mind is completely barren. So, whoever is aware of any spiritual decay must do a severe trial and examination of themselves to test their Christianity and obedience. These decays show temporary faith, and it is only real faith that thrives and grows to the end. Those who have this faith will bear fruit as promised and be free from such declines.

This spiritual life that abides, thrives, and grows to the end is testified in three ways in the Bible.

It Grows

It is compared to things that increase and progress without fail. Its growth is often likened to well-watered plants and trees in fruitful soil that will always grow unless some external violence occurs. It is also compared to those things whose progress is absolutely infallible: "But the path of the righteous is like the light of dawn, which shines brighter and brighter until full day" (Prov. 4:18). The path of the just is his covenant-walk before God, as it is often called in the Bible, comprising the principle, profession, and fruits of it (Ps. 119:35, Isa. 26:7, Ps. 23:3, Matt. 3:3, Heb. 12:13). The wise man says this is like the morning light. Why is it like this? Because it progresses bit by bit, shining more and more until noon. This path of the just: goes on and increases to its noon, the perfect day of glory. It is in its nature to do this, even though it can sometimes be obstructed, as we will see later, just like the morning light.

There is no visible difference between the light of the morning and the light of the evening. Sometimes the rays of the setting sun look more glorious than the other. But there is a difference: the morning light gradually goes on until it reaches perfection, and the other gradually gives way to darkness, until it is midnight. It is the same with the light of the just and of the hypocrite. At first, they may seem the same and equal, convictions and spiritual gifts working in some hypocrites, illuminating their declaration more than the grace of those properly born again. But here they discover their different natures: the one increases and goes on constantly, though it may sometimes be faintly, while the other decays, grows dim, and becomes darkness and crooked walking.

This is the path of the just. If our walk before God is different from this, there will be no evidence that we are on that path, or that we have a living, growing spiritual life in us. All Christians should be aware of these things because it is hidden under physical degeneration. Love of the world, conformity to it, neglect in spiritual duties, and coldness in spiritual love are evidence of these declines. But let no one deceive themselves: wherever there is a living grace, it will be thriving and growing to the end. And if there are obstacles that bring deterioration for a season, it will bring no rest or peace to the soul but will continually strive for recovery. Peace in a spiritually decaying condition is a soul-ruining security. It is better to be afraid of falling into sin than be in peace in the decay of spiritual life.

Comparing the path of the just to the morning light is like the light that appeared to the world, and then, after a season, because of clouds and storms, gave way again to darkness like the night. But it has not been lost and buried. After a while, it recovered to a greater brilliance than before and increased while it was eclipsed. It is like this for many who are just born again. They have huge darkness and trouble through Satan's efficient temptations that possessed their minds, but the grace that receded, like the morning light, has disentangled itself and revealed it was far from being extinguished as it grew and thrived under all those clouds and darkness. The light of the just always increases during temptations, while the hypocrite is constantly weakened by them.

As the morning light has a definite progress, Jesus calls it "living water" and "a spring of water welling up to eternal life" (John 4:10, 14). It is a spring that does not fail—not a pool or pond that dries up. Many pools of light, gifts, and declarations have completely dried up when people grow older or are trapped by the temptations of the world. We see others under dangerous decays every day; their faces change, and they have lost that oil that makes the face of a Christian shine—the oil of love, humility, self-denial, and spirituality. Instead, there is an ointment of pride, self-love, earthly mindedness, which increases. But where this principle of spiritual life is, it is like the morning light, an unfailing spring that flows in eternal life.

Promised to Grow

There are promises given to Christians about this, to strengthen them with grace to help their spiritual life grow, increase, and flourish to the end as we have seen in Psalm 92. These promises are the way this spiritual life is revealed and transmitted to us and preserved in us. They make us participants of this divine nature, and it continues in us through them (2 Pet. 1:4). The promises are of this nature, that by the gift of the Spirit, and supplies of his grace, our spiritual life will flourish, and be fruitful to the end, are written in the Bible:

I will pour water on the thirsty land, and streams on the dry ground I will pour my Spirit upon your offspring; and my blessing on your descendants. They shall spring up among the grass like willows by flowing streams. (Isa. 44:3-4)

Although this promise is about God dealing graciously with the Jews after their return from captivity, it also speaks of the redemption of the church by Jesus. It belongs to the Gospel when the righteous were to flourish, and it is a promise of the new covenant given to believers but is also extended to their children—a sign of new covenant promises.

1. Before and after our conversion to God, we are like thirsty, dry, and barren ground. We have nothing in ourselves, no radical moisture to make us flourish and be fruitful. "Not that we are sufficient in ourselves to claim anything as

coming from us, but our sufficiency is from God" (2 Cor. 3:5). Being left to ourselves, we will wither and die.

2. God brings relief in this case; he will pour the sanctifying water of his Spirit and the blessing of his grace upon us. He will do it to make us spring up like the grass, as willow trees by the river. There is nothing more renowned for its growth than willows near water. This is what the spiritual growth of Christians under these promises will be like—fat and flourishing, bearing fruit. There are many similar promises, but we must observe three things:

   a. The promises of the new covenant, through the gift of grace, are absolute and unconditional. They are the executive transmission of God's indisputable purposes and decrees. What is the condition of receiving this grace? The glory of covenant promises, imparting the grace of conversion and sanctification to Christians, is absolutely free and unconditional.

   b. The promises of growth and measures of this grace in us are not the same. There are many duties required of us, that these promises may be accomplished in us—diligence in obedience is expected from us in this (2 Pet. 1:4–10). This is the ordinary method of transmission of all grace to make us spiritually flourish and be fruitful—to diligently exercise what we have received. God sometimes deals with us in other ways through his sovereignty, surprising us with healing grace in the midst of our decays and backsliding (Isa. 57:17-18). In this way, many poor souls have been delivered from going down into the pit. The good shepherd will go out of his way to save a wandering sheep, but this is the ordinary method.

c. Despite these promises of growth, flourishing, and fruitfulness, if we are negligent in improving in the grace we have received and carrying out the duties required, we may backslide and remain in a low, unhealthy state. This is the main difference between the glory and beauty of the church, as shown in the promises of the Gospel and as exemplified in the lives of Christians—they do not live up to the condition of their accomplishment in them, but in God's way and time, they will be all fulfilled. So, we have many promises concerning the thriving, growing, and flourishing of the spiritual life in us, even in old age and until death, but the grace promised for this will not come to us while we are asleep in spiritual laziness and false security. Fervent prayer, the exercise of all grace received, with vigilance in all Christian duties, is required.

Growth Is of God

God has secured the growth of this spiritual life by providing food to strengthen and increase it because life must be preserved by food. We see this in the Bible with all other commands of worship that depend on it (1 Pet. 2:2-3). Whatever the state of life is—its beginning, its progress, its decay—there is proper sustenance provided in the Word of God's grace. If people neglect the daily food provided for them, they will become weak and useless. And if Christians are not sincere in their desire for this food—not diligent in it or seeing it as worthless as common food—they will fall into spiritual decline. But God has provided this for our growth even into old age.

The spiritual life should be strong and reliable to be able to thrive and grow even in old age and to the end.

Danger of Decay

Despite the nature of spiritual life, Christians are still subject to many decays, partly gradual and partly by unpredictable temptations, which obstruct growth and dishonor the gospel so they lose their peace with joy.

And these spiritual decays are of two sorts.

1. Such as are gradual and universal, in the loss of the vigor and life of grace, both in its principle and in its excellence.
2. Such as are occasioned by surprise into sin through the power of temptation; I mean such sins as do waste the spiritual powers of the soul and deprive it of all solid peace.

As for temporary believers, give them but time enough in this world, especially if it be accompanied by outward prosperity or persecution, and, for the most part, their decays of one sort or another will make a discovery of their hypocrisy. Though they retain a form of godliness, they deny the power of it (Prov. 1:31, 2 Tim. 3:5). And if they do not openly relinquish all duties of religion, yet they will grow so lifeless and savorless in them, as will reveal evidence of their condition; for so it is with those who are lukewarm, who are neither hot nor cold, who have a name to live but are dead.

Here, we see a significant difference between sincere believers and those who believe only for a while. The second type either does not perceive their sickness and decline—their minds are filled with other things—or they are not concerned about their dry state, and when they are convicted, they cry, "A little sleep, a little slumber, a little folding of the hands to rest" (Prov. 24:33). But when real believers find anything of this nature, it makes them restless for a recovery. And because there are many snares, temptations, and deceits of sin, or through their ignorance of the proper ways, they do not all recover quickly, yet none of them stay in that condition or turn to any false cures.

The Bible shows that, as Christians, we are subject to these decays through the loss of our first faith, love, and works, the weakening of the of spiritual life, the loss of delight, joy, and consolation, and the decline of the fruits of obedience, which Jesus Christ charges five of the seven churches of Asia with (Rev. 2-3). In Sardis and Laodicea, the decay had reached a point where they were in danger of being rejected. This answers the experience of all churches and Christians in the world. Those who have a different attitude and mind are dead in sin and have lied to themselves in their miserable condition. This is how it is with religious state churches.

As for the second sort, where people are caught by unsuspecting temptations that produce huge spiritual distress and anguish, sensing God's displeasure, we have the example of David:

O Lord, rebuke me not in your anger, nor discipline me in your wrath! For your arrows have sunk into me, and your hand has come down on me. There is no soundness in my flesh because of your indignation; there is no health in my bones because of my sin. For my iniquities have gone over my head; like a heavy burden, they are too heavy for me. My wounds stink and fester because of my foolishness... (Ps. 38:1–10)

This is a description of a terrible state and condition. David knew he was called by God to be a teacher and instructor of the church for all ages, so he recorded his own experience for this reason. This is why it has the title: "A Psalm of David, for the memorial offering." Some people say David had a disease that came upon him, but if that was true, it was only a symptom of his complaint—the cause of it was sin. There are four things he shows here:

1. He had departed from God and fallen into provoking sins, which brought despair to his mind (v. 3-4).
2. He had foolishly continued in that state, not looking to grace and mercy for healing, so he became worse (v. 5). This is what makes such a

condition dangerous—when people do not quickly apply healing remedies.
3. He had a continual sense of God's displeasure because of sin (v. 2-4).
4. He was restless in this state, mourning, groaning, and striving for deliverance.

This is a clearer picture of the condition of Christians when the magnitude of any sin or persisting in a careless attitude brings them to feel God's displeasure. This opens their minds and hearts to reveal how they are inside, which they cannot deny. It is not like this with many as it was with David, even though he had huge public failures, the substance of this decline is found in all of them. The heart knows its own bitterness—no one knows the groaning and laboring of a soul convinced of such spiritual decays but the person carrying them. It is brought low, mourning the whole day, even though others know nothing of its sorrows. However, it is worse to see people who show their inner decline through their outward fruits, but they are hardly concerned about it. Real Christians are in recovery, but those who ignore their state are on the path down to death.

There are some Christians who have walked in the ways of the just for a long time and faced the temptations of life, but they have fallen asleep as the spouse complains (Song. 5:2). They have been overwhelmed with the decay of one sort or another, either spiritually or morally—in their churches or families, in their judgments or their desires, in their inner selves or outward actions—they have been overcome with laziness, negligence, or lacking diligence in faith. I wish it was not like this.

I want to look at those gradual declines in the life and power of grace that Christians fall into. These happen in the formality of holy duties, their performance of them, intense involvement in the affairs of life, an overestimation of sinful enjoyments, growth in worldly wisdom, neglect of daily putting to death the sins people are inclined to, and being secretly influenced by temptations of the days we live in.

A Common Condition

Many Christians have succumbed to spiritual decay and have no interest in the promise given.

I hope to bring conviction to them that needs some diligence. The glory of Christ, the honor of the Gospel, and the danger of people's souls call for it. This is the secret root of all our evil, which will not be removed unless it is dug up. Who cannot see, who does not complain of the loss or decay of the power of Christianity today? But there are few who know or apply themselves or others to the proper remedy of this evil. Besides, it is almost as difficult to convince people of their spiritual decay as it is to recover them from it. But without this, healing is impossible. If people do not know their sickness, they will not look for a cure. Some, when they see their sickness and their wound, will apply themselves incorrectly with useless remedies (Hos. 5:13). No one will use a cure if they do not see any disease at all. So, to bring a conviction to their minds, we might make use of some of the following observations.

Are You Aware of Decay?

In your Christianity, have you had any experience of these spiritual decays? I do not doubt that there are some who have been kept green and flourishing from the day they were born again, never falling into laziness, neglect, or temptation, at least not for long periods. But there are only a few people like this. It was also rare for any of those believers in the Old Testament whose lives are recorded for our instruction, and those who lived in diligent self-denial. There are those who gained relief and deliverance, whose backsliding was healed, and their diseases cured. So, it was with David:

Bless the Lord, O my soul, and all that is within me, bless his holy name! ... who forgives all your iniquity, who heals all your diseases, who redeems your life from the pit, who crowns you with steadfast love and mercy, who satisfies you with good so that your youth is renewed like the eagle's. (Ps. 103:1–5)

He celebrates his deliverance from that state that he complains about in Psalm 38. There is no grace or mercy that affects the hearts of believers more or gives them greater joy and thankfulness than being delivered from backsliding. Bringing the soul out of prison enlarges us to praise (Ps. 142:7). I do not doubt there are many like this because God has warned about the danger of a spiritually decaying state many times, and he has made great promises of recovery from it, and many in the church experience this every day. But I am speaking generally to everyone. Have you experienced such spiritual decay, either in your spirits or in your walking before God? Or are you prone to them, preserved by the power of grace in your own diligence? If not, then I am afraid it might be from one of these two causes:

1. You have never had any flourishing spiritual state in your souls. The person who has always been weak and sickly does not know what it is to lack health and strength, because they never experienced it; much less do those who are dead know what it is to lack life. But those who were very healthy and fell ill, know clearly how it was and how it is now. Regarding the attitude of many Christians in the way they live, if they are not aware of spiritual decay, it is evident that they never had any good spiritual health, and there is no reason to talk to them about a recovery. Among those who are superficial Christians, many live in all sorts of sins. If you tell them about backsliding, decay, and recovery, you will be like Lot with his sons-in-law. When he told them of the destruction of Sodom, they thought he was mocking them (Gen. 19:14). Or you will be mocked in return for telling them.

These people have always been that way; it has never been different, and it is ridiculous to speak to them about a recovery. We must be able to say to them, "Remember therefore from where you have fallen; repent, and do the works you did at first" (Rev. 2:5). They must have experienced a better state, or they will not make an effort to recover from the state they are in. Since they see no evil or danger in their present condition, supposing everything is well, because it is as good as ever it was, they will not be easily convicted. They need to question whether they have had anything of the truth of grace or not.

2. If you have not experienced this, then unfortunately you are asleep in self-confidence which is not much different from death in sin. The church of Laodicea had a backslide. It had gone away from its first faith and obedience, yet was so secure in its condition, knew so little about it, that it judged itself to be in a thriving, flourishing state. It thought it had increased in all church riches—gifts and grace—but was actually "wretched, pitiable, poor, blind, and naked" (Rev. 3:17). It was in such a state that it is questionable whether it had anything of the life and power of grace to be found in it or not. It is like this with many churches today, especially those that boast about being without error or blame. It is strange that a church should suppose it is flourishing in grace and gifts when it has nothing but the noise of words in its place.

So, God testified about Ephraim that "gray hairs are sprinkled upon him, and he knows it not" (Hos. 7:9). He was in a declining, dying condition, but did not understand it. It also says that "they do not return to the Lord their God, nor seek him, for all this" (v. 10). If people do not learn and own their spiritual decay, there is no hope of persisting with them to return to the Lord. "Those who are well have no need of a physician, but those who are sick;" Jesus "came not to call the righteous, but sinners" (Matt. 9:12-13). Such people are under the power of senseless security, and it is very hard to wake them up from it. So, we have little success in calling people to look for a revival and recovery from their decays. They say there is no such thing in them, and that it is for others. If anyone says something that upsets them, they think it was spoken out of spite toward them. They are fine in their present condition. This is the same complaint Jesus had when he preached the Word:

I have called and you refused to listen, have stretched out my hand and no one has heeded, because you have ignored all my counsel and would have none of my reproof. (Prov. 1:24-25)

Let this truth be said a thousand times because only one out of a thousand will think they need to be saved and recovered. A spirit of slumber and sleep seems to be poured over many.

Did You Have Spiritual Joy and Peace Before?

To emphasize this conviction, I would ask whether you have been able to maintain spiritual peace and joy in your soul. I take it for granted that these are inseparable from the life of faith, in a humble, fruitful walk before God, because the Bible says so and their experience backs it up. These people know what they are and do not delude themselves with fantasies: they have substance in them, even though they are mocked or unknown. Has this peace and joy been maintained in your mind? Through trials and temptations, have they been calm and unshaken or are you often uneasy and confused? A decaying spiritual state and solid spiritual peace do not go together, and if ever you had such peace, then losing it will reveal what state you are in.

Can You See Obvious Decay?

While people can justify themselves when it comes to internal and hidden things, there are also too many open, public displays of backsliding among Christians that the church and the world can see. Pride, selfishness, worldliness, unsuitable clothing, and vanity of life, with corrupt, unsavory talk are found among many of them. The world was never in a worse posture for conformity than it is at this day, wherein all flesh has corrupted its way; and yet, as to things of outward appearance, how little distinction is left between it and those who would be esteemed more strict professors of religion! Was this the way and manner of the saints of old—of those that went before us in the same profession? Was it so with ourselves in the time of our first espousals, when we went after God in the wilderness in a land that was not sown (Jer. 2:2)? Some understand what I say: if we have not, some of us, had better days, we never had good days in our lives; if we have had them, why do we not stir up ourselves to look after recovery?

Are You Tired of Serving God?

May God not say the same thing about us that he said about the Israelites, "You have been weary of me, O Israel!" (Isa. 43:22). Have we ever been weary of God so that we become weary of ourselves? Most people will respond by asking, "How or where have we been weary or tired of God?" Are we not busy doing duties of his service? What more is required of us? How are we to blame? People become tired of God when they get tired of him in their duties and services (Isa. 1:13-14). God says that he is weary: they say in their hearts that they are weary (Mal. 1:13).

But this excuse does not stand. Their laziness, indifference, and negligence in their Christian duties, both private and public, are notorious. Family prayer is neglected by many, and even if it is done, it is without consistency or passion. It might be grounded in the light of nature, confirmed by biblical rules, essential for families dedicated to God, strengthened by the constant example of those in the Bible, and necessary for those who walk with God; yet many do not have any argument or reason why they do not do it. Everything these Christians use to teach their children and servants is filled with the fruits of negligence. God has severely rebuked many of us for these shortfalls. Even in public worship of God, laziness and indifference are shown by many.

People can become tired of God while they carry out their Christian duties.

They can be like this with spirituality and focusing on the exercise of all grace, which is required for such duties. These are the life and soul, and without any external performance of them, it is a dead corpse. People draw close to God with their lips, but their hearts are far from him. "God is spirit, and those who worship him must worship in spirit and truth" (John 4:24) he is not for those people, but only in the exercise of the graces of his Spirit, because "bodily training is of some value, godliness is of value in every way" (1 Tim. 4:8).

To stay in the right attitude, we must motivate ourselves to constantly and passionately carry out our Christian duties, which require spiritual diligence and alertness. Pay attention to prayer. A thousand excuses come against it—all kinds of laziness, formality, exhaustion, and busy lifestyles rise up to frustrate this. Naturally, we are happy to rest, satisfied with the physical work done, thinking they are enough. But it would be better if we did not do them at all because our consciences will show us our condition. This will require lots of spiritual effort and diligence.

The external performance of Christian principles, however strictly followed like religious zealots, is an easy task—less than the amount of work some people do in their jobs. In performing these public and personal duties, people become tired of God: and according as they are remiss in the constant keeping up of spirituality, and the exercise of grace in sacred duties, so is the degree of their weariness. There is no clearer way to measure the decays or growth in the spirit, than in their attitudes when carrying out these duties. If they constantly stir themselves up to take hold of God (Isa. 64:7), it is evidence of good spiritual health in the soul. But this will not be done without vigilance and care against the influences of the flesh and other temptations. Laziness and formality are a sign of a dry inner state.

These people also carry out the external duties of Christianity but continue in sin. There is nothing of

God in those duties which do not involve putting sin to death. They have a form of godliness, tolerating the neglect of its power. If sin is indulged, denying it is not properly followed. If our Christian duties are not used, applied, and pointed in that direction, there is a weariness of God in them. Then the soul has no real communion or intimacy with God in them.

Do You Examine Yourself?

If we take a good look at the state of our souls and the spiritual characteristics that are useful, drawing us closer to the glory of God, many of us would be lacking. We are talking about passion, humility, repentance, spiritual-mindedness, strength, delight in God's ways, love, generosity, self-denial, and others like this. Are we fat and flourishing in these things, even in old age? Are they in us, and do they abound (2 Pet. 1:8)? Do we bear their fruit, showing the faithfulness of God in his supply of grace? Let us look at them, but I will only give two general rules to test ourselves in these.

1. Having no spiritual appetite for the food of our souls is evidence of a decay in all these things. Spiritual appetite is found in sincerely desiring and relishing the taste of it, which is why Peter says, "Like newborn infants, long for the pure spiritual milk, that by it you may grow up into salvation—if indeed you have tasted that the Lord is good." (1 Pet. 2:2-3). This spiritual appetite needs to desire the Word, built on an experience of God's grace in it, so we can grow and thrive spiritually. This appetite will give us a measure of the state of grace in us as a natural

appetite does with healthy food to bring health to the body.

Does this live in us as it did in those first days of being born again? We hear the Word preached, but do we have the same desire and spiritual relish as before? Some listen to satisfy their convictions, some to please their fancies, and some to judge those preaching it. Only a few are prepared to receive it for themselves.

When people grow old, they lose their natural appetite for food. They must still eat to keep them alive, but not because they desire it as they did when they were young and healthy. They think that the meat which they used to have was tastier than what they are now given, even though what they now enjoy is better. The change is in themselves. So, there are many Christians who think and say that the preaching they had in early days and the spiritual exercises they were engaged in were far better than what they now enjoy. But the change is in themselves—they have lost their spiritual appetite or their hunger and thirst after the food of their souls.

"One who is full loathes honey, but to one who is hungry everything bitter is sweet" (Prov. 27:7). People who have grown full of themselves and are proud of their own abilities have lost their spiritual appetite for the Word of God. This makes the Word lose its power in them. That Word that is "sweeter also than honey and drippings of the honeycomb" (Ps. 19:10) has little or no taste for them. If they were hungry, they would find sweetness in the most bitter rebukes instead of what they can now find in the sweetest promises. They come to hear the Word with sick desires and low expectations as if they were invited to eat at the end of a feast, being self-full before. This loss of spiritual appetite is evidence of the decay of all other Christian characteristics.

2. Not making Christianity our priority is another piece of evidence of the decay in us. Where grace is working, everything else ranks lower than our faith, as David declares twenty times in Psalm 119. Everything must come second. The love and value of it will consume our minds, thoughts, and emotions. The practice of it will bring order to all our other concerns. But for many, it is not this way: religion is just one of the things—everything else is preferred above it, and it cannot find any place in their minds. To see people continually plodding in the affairs of the world and adjusting all their actions to them, only diverting to Christian duties every so often, is not giving their faith a priority. There is no clearer evidence of backsliding than this one: that people do not make their belief in Jesus their main business. A little self-examination will help them judge what they make it to be.
3. Lastly, I might also point out the uselessness of people in their faith: they lack love for other Christians, have no good works, are not willing to obey the calls of God to repentance and change, and they love the world and are proud. These are all undeniable evidence that these people have never had any true grace at all and have suffered a backslide.

This is the third thing that was proposed—an effort to convict some people of their spiritual decline and the necessity for a revival. It is mainly for those of us who, having been Christians a long time, are now getting older and do not have much time left. And the truth is, I do not meet many Christians who have considerable experience and are spiritually minded but are not aware of the danger of backsliding in temptation. They know how difficult it is to keep up a vibrant, active attitude in faith, love, holiness, and fruitfulness. For those who are not concerned about this, I do not know what to make of them or their faith.

Recovering From Decay

People can be delivered from such decays and find the grace promised here so they can flourish spiritually in old age, strengthening their inner life and abounding in fruits of obedience, which are to the praise of God by Jesus. Then we will apply these truths in the next section.

Recognize There Is Hope

The state of spiritual decay is recoverable. No one who has experienced a backslide has any reason to say, "There is no hope!" as long as they take the right way to recovery. If every step that is lost toward heaven is irretrievable, there is no hope for us—we will all perish. If there is no restoration of our violations, no healing of our decays, no salvation except for those always progressing in grace; if God marks all that is done as wrong, as the Psalmist says, "O Lord, who should stand?", if we had no rescues each day, we remain in perpetual backsliding.

What is required is that we use the right method for recovery, not those which are destructive. When trees grow old or are decaying, it is useful to dig around them and fertilize them. This can help them to flourish again and bear fruit. But instead, if you take them out of the soil to plant them somewhere else, they will wither and die. It is the same with Christians. Finding themselves in decline, with little or nothing of the life and power of Christianity left in them, they have grown tired and have changed their soil or turned from one religion to another. They blame the religion, but the fault was only in themselves. There are many who wither and die this way. But if they used the proper methods for their healing and recovery, they might have lived and brought forth fruit.

Do It in His Power

Diligently denying oneself and obedience in Christian practice is required for recovery. These things are naturally the first relief in this case and should not be left out.

No rituals or duties of self-denial should be followed to try to find recovery from spiritual decay except those commanded by God. Anything else is strictly forbidden, no matter the excuse given. "Who has required this from your hand?" (Isa. 1:12 NKJV). Religious churches have invented works, ways, and duties to bring about self-denial, just like the Pharisees—God never appointed, nor approved, nor will accept these; nor will they ever do good for people's souls. Examples of these are confessions, disciplines, pilgrimages, set fasting, abstinence, and formal prayers to be repeated at specific times. The physical effort in these things brings no spiritual advantage.

But it is natural for people to turn to these routines to find relief. Those who are thoroughly convinced of spiritual decays are compelled by a sense of guilt because it is sin which has brought them into that condition. So, they try man-made techniques to atone God's displeasure and find his acceptance. If they are not under the actual conduct of evangelical light, two things will present themselves. First, they will engage in extraordinary obligations that God has not commanded. This is how they end up in ultra-religious churches where guilt, the darkness of corrupted nature, calls for it. Secondly, an extraordinary increase in those normal duties that we are required to do.

With what shall I come before the Lord, and bow myself before God on high? Shall I come before him with burnt offerings, with calves a year old? Will the Lord be pleased with thousands of rams, with ten thousands of rivers of oil? Shall I give my firstborn for my transgression, the fruit of my body for the sin of my soul? (Micah 6:6-7)

They hope these methods will bring restitution to their condition. There are two types of spiritual decay: first, from the power of convictions which are multiplied in temporary Christians; and, secondly, from degrees in the power of saving grace. Those who have the first kind are never diverted from attempting to find relief this way, and when they fail, they stop trying and let themselves go in their lusts because they have no light of the gospel to guide them.

The second type makes every effort to recover from backsliding and thrive in grace by concerted attention to denying themselves and new obedience. But they must be careful that it is of God and that the way they do this lines up with the Bible. These consist of constant reading and hearing of the Word, passionate prayer, and being alert against temptations and sin. They must try, through holy sincerity and rebuking wrong attitudes, to keep the mind spiritual and heavenly in its thoughts and desires.

They must be careful not to attempt these things in their own strength. When people have strong convictions about fulfilling a duty, they are prone to do it in their own strength. They must do them; they will do them—external work—they think they can do them. The Holy Spirit rejects this confidence—no one will prosper this way (2 Cor. 3:5, 9:8). But many deceive themselves, laboring in the fire, while all they do immediately is perish. They have been negligent and careless, and that peace which they had is compromised. But now, they will pray, read, fast, give to the poor, and turn from sin. They think they can do this all by themselves because they perform works as duties require.

When this is done, Jesus is left out because, when all is done, it is the Lord that heals us (Exod. 25:26). There is another evil here: whatever people do in their natural abilities, there is a secret pride in it. Those who defend this, say there can be no good in anything except what comes from our own free will. This is enough to make all efforts of this kind not only useless and fruitless but completely rejected. Faith needs the assistance of Jesus and his grace in these duties, otherwise, they will not be effective for our healing and recovery, no matter how often we do them. We use and do them according to the supply of grace from above and in the work of faith.

Hold Onto His Promises

The work of recovering backsliders or believers from their spiritual decline is an act of sovereign grace, through God's promises. Out of this eater comes meat. Believers are liable to this declines, backsliding, and decay, so God has provided and given to us great and precious promises of recovery if we apply ourselves to them. One example of this in the Bible is worth looking at here:

Return, O Israel, to the Lord your God, for you have stumbled because of your iniquity. Take with you words and return to the Lord; say to him, "Take away all iniquity; accept what is good, and we will pay with bulls the vows of our lips. I will heal their apostasy; I will love them freely, for my anger has turned from them. I will be like the dew to Israel; he shall blossom like the lily; he shall take root like the trees of Lebanon; his shoots shall spread out; his beauty shall be like the olive, and his fragrance like Lebanon. They shall return and dwell beneath my shadow; they shall flourish like the grain; they shall blossom like the vine; their fame shall be like the wine of Lebanon. O Ephraim, what have I to do with idols? It is I who answer and look after you. I am like an evergreen cypress; from me comes your fruit. (Hos. 14:1–8)

It talks about the disease and remedy in the experience of the church, and God's dealing with them. We can find many simple directions from this passage and guidance in our progress.

When God said, *"Return, O Israel,"* it was to those who were wicked and were devoted to complete destruction. This is shown in the chapter before, and then we see that their desolation came soon after. There are no seasons or circumstances that can obstruct sovereign grace when God administers it to his church—it works in the midst of heavy judgment.

God's chosen people of Israel were often overcome by sin, backsliding from God and falling into spiritual decay. It was the same story here, even though they had not completely broken the covenant with God. He was still *"The LORD thy God"* to them, but they had fallen into iniquity. Public backsliding is often accompanied by partial defects: "Because lawlessness will be increased, the love of many will grow cold" (Matt. 24:12).

When God comes to heal his people from backsliding by sovereign grace, he gives them clear calls to repentance and this method for their healing: *"Take with you words and return to the Lord."* If God stirred up his faithful ministers to strongly insist all the people do their duty in this and let them know that there is no other way to prevent their destruction but by returning to the Lord, then it is clear that the time of healing was at hand.

Repent

The method given to heal our backsliding in a way that

is suitable to the glory of God is renewed repentance. This is done in the following ways:

1. **Fervent prayer.** *"Take with you words."* Consider the importance of the work before you and that you are dealing with God. There are two parts to the subject of this prayer.
   a. The forgiveness of sin. Taking it all away, where no sin is left, all of it equally heavy. *"Take away all iniquity."* When sinners are sincere in their return to God, they will not leave one sin out. We are not fit for healing, nor will we apply ourselves properly, without some previous sense of God's love in the forgiveness of our sins.
   b. Gracious acceptance. *"Receive us graciously."* The words in the original are *"accept what is good,"* but both have the same meaning: *"Receive us graciously."* After we have thrown ourselves under your displeasure, now let us know that we are freely accepted by you. This is the desire of those who want to receive healing from their backsliding because they are aware that God is not pleased if they remain there.
2. **Confessing sins.** Acknowledging those sins that have caused backsliding. *"Assyria shall not save us;"*—*"we will say no more, 'Our God,' to the work of our hands"* (v. 3). Self-confidence and false worship were the two great sins that ruined these people. These believers allowed these sins as we have with the current sins of our days by conforming to the world. God

expects a full confession of these sins in order to be healed.

3. **Renewed commitment.** Rejecting all other hopes and expectations and putting their complete trust and confidence in him. They first express the cause which was his grace and mercy—*"In you the orphan finds mercy"*—and, secondly, the effect if praise and thanksgiving, *"the vows of our lips."*

   a. Although God will repair our spiritual decay and heal our backsliding, he will do it in a way so he can impart grace to us to the praise of his own glory. These duties are given to us because even though they are not the reason we receive love and grace that heal us, they are still the method through which he pours out his grace. There is no better example of the consistency and harmony between sovereign grace and diligence in our duties than in this verse: As God promises he would heal their backsliding out of his free love (v. 4) and would do it by imparting his grace (v. 5), so he tells them to carry out these duties.

   b. Unless these things are worked in us to prepare us to receive this mercy, we have no firm expectation that we will participate in it. This is how God deals with the church. We can expect a gracious revival from all our decay when serious repentance is found in us. This grace will not surprise us in our laziness, negligence, and false security, but it comes by stirring us up to sincere efforts in our duties. Until we see better evidence of this repentance among us than we have now, we have no real hope of recovery.

Meditate on Grace

The work is shown in the following:

1. **By its nature.** *"I will heal their apostasy."* Its nature is healing backsliding from the sin that has caused them to fall from God, and now it encourages them to return. Sin brings souls into a diseased state and danger of death: the cure for this is God's work. That is why he gives himself the title, "I am the LORD, your healer" (Exod. 15:26). Because of the poisonous nature of sin and the danger it brings of eternal death to people's souls, removing it or recovering from it is often called healing (Ps 6:2, Isa. 57:18-19, Hos. 6:1). In this healing, we see two things: first, the pardon of past sins; and then, grace to make us fruitful in obedience: *"I will be like the dew to Israel."* This is God's healing of backsliding.
2. **In its causes.** This is the main cause: free, undeserved love. *"I will love them freely."* We can expect recovery from this alone. There is also the efficient cause, which is pardoning mercy: *"my anger has turned from them;"* and renewed obedience that comes with an abundance of grace: *"I will be like the dew to Israel."* Fresh supplies of the Spirit of grace are necessary for our healing and recovery.

3. **By its effect.** There is a more abundant fruitfulness in holiness and obedience in peace and love than they ever had before. The prophet describes this in many metaphors to show the greatness and power of the grace that is imparted.

The Reason for These Words

Now that we have looked at the opening verses, I want to look specifically at each part as it is clearly represented. By this, we will see the following:

First, how the exercise of faith helps us obtain this grace.

Secondly, how wonderful it is to have our spiritual decay and backsliding healed so grace can work in our spiritual lives with flourishing Christianity and fruitful obedience (even in old age). The Holy Spirit reveals the beauty and glory of this work of love, mercy, and grace to the glory of God. Our duties and practices are not easy or common, but for those of us who participate, they are life from the dead.

Third, that no one will completely lose hope because of their decay. When people are awakened by new convictions and begin to feel the weight of them and how entangled they are, they are ready to give up and despair of deliverance. But here we see a promise of deliverance through pardoning mercy and also of fresh springs of grace that cause us to abound in holiness and fruitfulness. Who is entangled with corruptions and temptations, that groans under a sense of a cold, lifeless, barren state of heart? They can find spiritual refreshment if they apply this promise in faith.

More Direction

We can have the fruit of this and all other promises like it. We can be flourishing and fruitful even in old age. I will give some directions about these methods that give life and power to all, and which bring us full enjoyment of this mercy:

1. **All From Him.** Our grace all comes from Jesus. Grace is spoken of in the promises of the Old Testament, but its impartation and our receiving of it, is revealed in the New Testament. This is part of its mystery: that all grace is from Christ, and it is useless to expect it any other way. He said "Apart from me you can do nothing,;" we cannot bear fruit on our own any more than a branch that is separated from the vine (John 15:3–5). He is our head, and all our spiritual influences—through the impartation of grace—are from him alone. He is our life efficiently and lives in us effectively so that our ability for important works is from him (Gal. 2:20, Col. 3:1–4). Are any of us under the conviction of spiritual decay? Do we long for the renovation of spiritual strength that makes us flourish in faith, love, and holiness? We must know that nothing can be attained, unless it comes from Jesus Christ alone. We see the promises and the duties given to us, but however we apply ourselves one way or the

other, they will bring no relief unless we know how to receive it from Jesus himself.
2. **Only by faith.** We can only receive spiritual strength and grace from Jesus by faith. This is how we come to him, are planted in him, and abide with him so we can bear fruit. He lives in our hearts by faith, he acts in us by faith, and we live by faith in the Son of God. If we receive anything from Christ, it must be by faith—it must be in the exercise of it or in believing. There is no verse in the Bible that encourages us to expect grace or mercy from him in any other way.
3. **Faith recognizes Jesus.** This faith respects the person of Jesus, his grace, his mediation, with all its effects, and his glory in them all. This is the issue: a steady view of the glory of Christ, in his person, grace, and work, through faith—a constant, lively exercise of faith in him, as he is revealed to us in the Bible—is the only way to find revival from our spiritual decay and obtain grace to make us flourish and be fruitful. The person who lives by faith in him, in spiritual thriving and growth, will "declare that the LORD is upright; he is my rock, and there is no unrighteousness in him" (Ps. 92:15).

To close this section, we can look at this as it is shown in the Bible and at the ways this grace or duty will produce this effect.

The Bible Testifies

We are told that "those who look to him are radiant, and their faces shall never be ashamed" (Ps. 34:5). It is Jesus, or the glory of God in him, that we look to—this no one will deny. And it is their faith which is expressed by looking to him which is seeing his glory as we have described. It is an act of trust that comes from knowing who and what he is. The effect of this is that they were enlightened—they received a fresh impartation of spiritual, saving, refreshing light from him, and of all other graces of which their faces were not ashamed. We will not fail in our expectation of new spiritual impartation if we have the same faith.

This is what we are called to do: "Turn to me and be saved, all the ends of the earth!" (Isa. 45:22). On this view of Jesus, his glory, our salvation depends. This is how we receive grace and glory. This is the direction given to us by the Holy Spirit to receive them.

We see it again: "But as for me, I will look to the Lord; I will wait for the God of my salvation; my God will hear me" (Micah 7:7). The church knew no other way of relief, no matter what it went through.

Seeing Jesus as crucified (and how glorious he was in it has been declared) is the cause and fountain of that godly sorrow, which is a spring of all other graces, especially in those who have fallen in decay (Zech. 12:10). It is also desiring strength from him to enable us to endure all our trials, troubles, and hardships with patience to the end (Heb. 12:2).

How We Are Changed

The only other thing to look at is how a constant view of Jesus' glory will produce this effect in us in different ways.

1. It will come from that transforming power that always accompanies this exercise of faith. This is what changes us every day more and more into the likeness of Christ. All revivals and flourishing are contained in this. To conform to Jesus is all we are capable of in this life; the perfection of it is eternal happiness. According to the measure of conformity we achieve, so is the thriving and flourishing of the life of grace in us which is what we aim for. Other ways and means, it may be, have failed us—let us put this to the trial. Let us live in the constant contemplation of the glory of Jesus and virtue will proceed from him to repair all our decay, to renew a right spirit within us, and to cause us to abound in all duties of obedience. Blood and flesh will not reveal these effects—it is like washing in the Jordan to cure leprosy, but the life of faith is a mystery known only to those who have it.
2. It will focus the soul on that object which can bring delight, peace, and satisfaction. This in perfection is happiness, because it is caused by the eternal vision of the glory of God in Jesus. The nearer we come to this state, the better, more spiritual, and more heavenly is the state of our souls. And we only get this from a constant contemplation of Jesus' glory.

a. Most of our spiritual decay and dryness comes from letting many other things into our minds because those weaken grace in its work. But when the mind is filled with thoughts of Jesus and his glory, when the soul clings to him with intense desire, they will throw out or not allow those causes of spiritual weakness (Col. 3:1–5, Eph. 5:8).
b. When we are busy in this duty, it will stir up every grace, which is spiritual revival. This is all we desire and long for, this will make us fat and flourishing—that every grace of the Spirit is worked in us (Rom. 5:3–5, 2 Pet. 1:5–8). Jesus is the first proper object of all grace, and all its work (for it first respects him, and then other things for him). When the mind is fixed on him and his glory, every grace will be ready to work. Without this, we will never gain it by any decisions or efforts of our own, try as much as we want.
c. This will make us vigilantly alert and in constant conflict against all the deceitful ways of sin, against all temptation, against all useless imaginations that cause our decay. Our recovery or revival will not happen, nor will a fresh spring of grace be found, in a careless, lazy Christianity. It requires constant watching and fighting against sin with our best efforts to beat it. Nothing will motivate and encourage our souls as a constant view of Jesus and his glory. Everything in him has a restraining

power over sin, as anyone who is acquainted with these things knows.

Study Guide - Reflections

This chapter starts off specifically targeting Christians who are getting old and who are slowing down in their spiritual fervor or losing their spark. One of the reasons is that Owen was in his 60s when he wrote this book. In fact, it was published shortly after he died. Experiencing the decay of the body and the simultaneous decay of the spirit, he obviously saw the need to warn and encourage older Christians in their final days. However, we should not skip over these pages if we do not have gray hair yet. The Gospel is no different for those who are grandparents than it is for grandchildren.

And so, this chapter is aimed at every believer who is keen to live better, more spirit-filled, by seeing the glory of Jesus. Owen's hope is that each one of us flourishes and grows in our walk with the Lord, that we take the path of the just, and that the glory of Jesus becomes our guiding light while we are on earth and when we are nearing heaven.

1. Why do the things we experience in our bodies affect our spiritual lives so much?
2. Why is death such an obstacle for many believers? Why should it not be a problem? Read 1 Corinthians 15:55-58
3. Do you struggle with fears and reluctance when it comes to death?

4. What are the things that stop us from flourishing as Christians? What are the things that hinder you in your life? What can you do about them?
5. Owen uses the word "conviction" a lot in these last two chapters—why is it important for us as Christians?
6. Self-denial is another critical aspect that he touches on. Why is it so important but seldom seen in Christians today? Read Matthew 16:24.

ABOUT JOHN OWEN

John Owen published around eight million words and was one of the most prolific Christian writers of his time. From poetry to politics, he wrote on many issues, although he is most famously known for his biblical teachings.

Born in 1616, Owen was educated at Queen's College in Oxford, going on to become a chaplain and tutor. As a staunch defender of Calvinism, he became famous for his doctrinal stand arguing against many false teachings that sprang up.

Despite this, he was closely linked with politics and became an advisor and supporter to Oliver Cromwell. Traveling with the statesman as he brought his sweeping changes to England, Owen was never shy to disagree to the point of petitioning against Cromwell becoming king. Later, he fell out of favor with those in power and focused on spiritual matters, leading him to write many of his later well-known works. His most celebrated was *Communion with God*, in which he helped Christians to relate to each person of the Trinity.

If there was one thing he was renowned for, it was his adherence to the Bible. As in *The Glory of Christ*, it is obvious that he relied heavily on Scripture to back his teachings. He believed that no Christian should choose between the Bible and the Spirit, but that the two should always go hand in hand.

Owen outlived his first wife and every one of his 11 children, most of whom died when they were young. He lived to the age of 67, leaving behind a wealth of Puritan writing that touched on so many issues.

BIBLIOGRAPHY

Crossway. (2001). *English Standard Version Bible*. Crossway Bibles.

Henderson, J. (n.d.). *Hadrian: Poem III*. Loeb Classical Library. https://www.loebclassics.com/view/hadrian-poems/1934/pb_LCL434.445.xml

Holman Bible Publishers. (2016). *The Holy Bible: NKJV New King James Version*. Holman Bible Publishers.

Owen, J. (1852). *The Person and Glory of Christ*. Robert Carter & Brothers.

Tyndale House Publishers. (2008). *NLT study Bible*. Tyndale House Pub.

www.ingramcontent.com/pod-product-compliance
Lightning Source LLC
LaVergne TN
LVHW020423070526
838199LV00003B/257